Screw Dog

Ivan Chicchon

D1359953

cheers!

-Ivan

DEDICATION

To my wife, Teresa. Here's to finding our *stability*.

ACKNOWLEDGMENTS

To my family who has are always there for me. To all the friends from whom I have learned valuable lessons along the way. To the Implant Ninja Team who gives everything to the mission. I can't thank you enough.

CHAPTER 1

"I'm going to drop out of dental school," I spoke into the phone.

Silence.

"I just don't think it's how I'm gonna build something great. I need to create something substantial, and that's not going to happen by spending all my time on.....*this*," I said, as I waved my hand toward the PowerPoint lecture I had been memorizing.

More silence.

Telling my fiancée that I was going to drop out of school was not exactly the smartest thing I could have done if I wanted her to actually go through with marrying me. Especially after I had already sunk a non-refundable $200k and the past 2 years into this.

But for the life of me, I couldn't figure out how dental school was getting me any closer to accomplishing my goal.

I have always wanted to create something, build something...what's the word...*worthy*? *Great?*

It started when I immigrated to the US with my parents. My mom was a housekeeper, and my dad made pizzas for Domino's during the week and on the weekends he stood by the curb outside of Home Depot, waiting for construction gigs.

Together on Saturday nights, we would go to a warehouse to assemble stacks of Sunday morning newspapers. They got paid by how many stacks they made. When the papers were folded and stacked, they resembled giant staircases to nowhere. One day after they refused to let me climb up this paper staircase, I got mad and kicked one over. It dominoed and ruined all their work for the evening.

They were dentists back in Peru. But here, we lived this hustle.

They worked odd jobs during the day and they studied at night. Working towards passing their US dental boards to become licensed dentists here in the states.

I was a scrappy little 7 year old kid when my parents got their letter in the mail containing their results from the exam.

"Pasamos!" They yelled! They had both passed. They gave each other a big kiss.

As I launched myself off of the couch and clung to them, I yelled, "Somos ricos!!!!" Which in Spanish meant, "We're rich!!!!"

We had finally made it. We celebrated with the complementary pepperoni pizza my dad brought home from work.

The next phase in my life was much different. Kids often told me, "Things must be so easy because your parents are dentists." And adults said things like, "You are sooo lucky."

Whenever me or my siblings would complain about a school exam, my dad would say,

"You think *this* is hard? Try taking the exam in a foreign language. Try studying on an empty stomach."

And my mom would chime in:

"Don't worry hijo, I took my dental board exam after spending the entire night in labor with your sister. You'll be fine."

I didn't know why, but we were constantly moving. Every 2 to 3 years in school, I would be the new kid with the funny last name.

The moment I dreaded the most was when the teacher would introduce me for the first time.

"Children, today we have a new face in the classroom. We have here, Mister Ivan...um...Chick...Ch...Chicken!"

The classroom would always burst into uncontrolled laughter.

Embarrassed, I would try to laugh along with them. Not surprisingly, some kids would carry this joke to the playground. Most were just having fun, but there was always one person who wanted to be a bully.

So, I learned to deal with bullies swiftly.

To be the most effective, I had to take care the situation immediately.

This was my bully-quashing checklist:

1. Step right up to them, toe-to-toe
2. Get in their faces (although I would usually only be as tall as their chest)
3. Don't blink, don't be the first to look away.
4. Threaten to clobber them with my fist (or with my Ziplock full of pogs)

The more aggressive the bully, the more crazy you'd have to be initially. They had to know that this little dude was nuts. They had to think that I was willing to take this spat to the next, next, next level.

It was sort of crazy but as my Macho Man Randy Savage poster said, "The best defense is a good offense." I probably took that one a bit too far.

But I also sought acceptance from the group, bullies and all. Never really fitting in, I wanted to impress my classmates.

"I know I just threatened to clobber you, but do you want to play Pogs?"

I always felt somehow apart. On the outside looking in.

So, from a very young age, I looked for ways to succeed on my own accord. To say, "Look at this everyone! I did this, I made this, I built this...and it is awesome."

Although I sought acceptance from my peers and from my parents, I think I actually sought acceptance from myself. I felt like I needed to earn my own approval. Permission to be proud of myself.

I think part of that came from my dad. He would often wake me and my brother and sister by throwing cold water on us from the doorway, saying, "Time to get up and get to work! We're not raising lazy kids!"

That became my inner voice.

We're not lazy. Get to work.

So I hustled.

I became the kid buying and selling beanie babies & Pokémon cards. I went door to door selling car wash services. One day I brought loaded dice to school (they were rigged to land on 7) and hustled classmates on the blacktop.

While my classmates watched Pokémon, I bought audio lesson cassettes titled "Negotiate Like the Pros" from the flea market...and then I watched Pokémon. I read business books and I also learned a lot from watching my parents as they built their dental business.

My parents were my ever present heroes. And they were complete opposites from one another.

My mom always encouraged me. She always wanted me to explore new things. She said things like, "You can do it hijo!"

She saw that I liked to take my time to do things meticulously so she took to calling me her "*tortuga ninja*" or ninja turtle.

Although she worked just as hard as my dad, she was also fully committed to finding ways for me to learn, grow, and be happy.

When I was 5 years old, my mom found out that the Power Rangers were coming to Florida, and she made sure we tracked them down. She climbed over tables and pushed her way through a crowd to make sure that we secured a spot right at the front of the line so I could proudly collect my autograph from the White Ranger.

Then when I was 12, she found out that my favorite WWF wrestler, Brett "The Hitman" Hart, was coming to California and just like before she made sure I got to meet my hero.

When I was obsessed with web design in 7th grade, she sent me to a coding bootcamp at Stanford University. In 8th grade when I told my mom that I wanted to become an Olympic wrestler, she found a wrestling club in a nearby city.

When she picked me up after my first day of practice, I hobbled over to the car. My face was scratched up and red, and my shirt was torn.

Thinking that I had a bad experience, my mom asked, "Ivancito, are you okay? Did you get hurt??"

My eyes lit up, "YEA! IT WAS AWESOME!!"

Then she sent me to an Olympic wrestling camp in Ohio.

She was always my biggest cheerleader. And aside from the bible verses she spoke to me on a daily basis, the quote that I most remember her telling me was from Sir Winston Churchill.

She read the highlighted text aloud from a book,

"Never give in. Never give in. Never, never, never, never—in nothing, great or small, large or petty – never give in except to convictions of honor or good sense."

Throughout my life, she was the embodiment of that quote.

Now my dad was a completely different animal.

He was always on beastmode. He worked harder and faster than anyone else and could be a bit rough around the edges. As a matter of fact, if you ever asked him to help you move furniture, you were in trouble. He was so fast and aggressive in his movements that he would, with 100% certainty, injure the person he was helping. If his own fingers got crunched or a dresser fell on his foot, it didn't seem to bother my dad. He was as tough as they came.

He also enjoyed life more than anyone else. You could always find him with a drill in his hands (dental drill or power drill) or with a Guitar, dancing as he played La Bamba. The way he lived his life told me, "You can enjoy life, as long as you earn it with your hands."

He was generous to a fault. Always giving, freely to friends, even if he had only just met them.

When I was a kid, I remember telling him that I would become a successful businessman. So, he took me on ridealongs with him to teach me business. He took me to the flea market and told me that if I wanted to learn business, "*real business*", all I had to do is watch people at the market. He said this is where you find people with "the eye of the tiger."

One day he took me to the dealership and allowed me to negotiate a car purchase on his behalf. He would be nonchalantly flipping through a magazine, while I haggled down the fees and options with the horrified car salesman who found himself negotiating with a kid.

As I sat in car with him on these ridealongs, he'd tell me "Your most valuable asset is your time. Never waste it, Ivancito."

He always pushed me, *dared me*, to do things. A constant source of ideas for hustles, he would say things like, "you should buy an air jumper and rent it out, you'll make tons of money!" or "you should buy a vending machine and distribute them around the city" or "I know a guy who did (fill in the blank), and now he is filthy rich!"

He would stare deep into your eyes as he enunciated the word *filthy*.

But my attempts to impress him always fell short. He always thought I should do more, accomplish more, be more.

So, I tried harder. And I tended to take things a bit too far.

Or, to "Go big or go home," as I often said to myself. That landed in me into some trouble, especially as I entered high school.

Right before I started my freshman year, we moved again.

This time to the farmlands of Central Valley California. To a city called Stockton where my parents had purchased a clinic from a retiring dentist. We didn't know it then, but Stockton would soon become labeled as "America's most miserable city." After the housing crash of '08, it became the biggest US city to go bankrupt. It would become notorious for homicides, home invasions, and robberies.

It was a tough city. But we didn't know that yet.

All I knew was that again, I was the new kid from another city, with the funny last name. If I hoped that the kids in high school would be more mature, the first day proved me wrong.

My immediate aggressive responses made the would-be bullies stand down and leave me alone.

But knowing nobody and having a big chip on my shoulder, I looked for ways to prove myself.

So I tried out for wrestling. On the first day of try outs, the guys made fun of my last name, pronouncing it as "chicken." When I beat everyone down and held my own against the upper classmen, they modified that nickname to "Crazy Chicken." As in "Don't mess with Chicken, he's crazy!" They soon became my second family.

When it came to matches and tournaments, my parents were always there to shout from the bleachers and to hug me as I walked off the mat. Although after a while it became too stressful for my mom to bear, so she would instead wait at home and get the details from me after. But my dad always made sure to follow me to every single event. He was always present to help me warm up before a match and to walk silently outside with me after a match.

Wrestling is an intense sport. Each round gives you 2 minutes to dominate your opponent, which meant that there was no down-time. You'd always hear shouts from the side of the mat saying, "EXPLODE!!" We were encouraged to "leave it all on the mat" – which meant that you should wrestle so hard that you shouldn't have any energy left over after a match.

When I was busy with wrestling, I didn't have time to cause trouble. But as soon as the off-season hit, I got restless. And looked for more hustles to occupy my time.

For instance, I found that I could steal things and then resell them at school. So, I organized a group of kids that would go with me to a store and we'd make a killing. Especially since I had fashioned a button down shirt with a hidden pocket in it that discretely transferred the stolen object down into a really large custom-sewn reservoir in my pants.

Of course my mom was the one who had taught me to sow. She probably wondered why I had taken on a sudden interest in tailoring clothes.

As I left the stores carrying the stolen loot, I had to walk in just the right way (sort of hunched over and with a slight limp) to avoid revealing this huge lump in my pants. But now that I think about it, walking like Quasimodo is not any less suspicious.

In another, now shameful venture, I started growing several marijuana plants in hopes of being a cannabis entrepreneur.

When my mom discovered my stash, she was crestfallen that her "Ivancito" would get mixed up in this.

She had always been there for me. When we were kids she had read us bible stories and taught us what it meant to be a good person and a good Christian. Her guidance did leave an impact on me. I wanted to do good things. I wanted to make a positive impact in the world.

But for a kid in high school, religious teachings just couldn't compete with popularity and fitting in with the tribe.

"Call the police" my dad ordered. "We have to teach our son a lesson." As I waited for the police to arrive, I got the bright idea to flush my prized possessions down the toilet. Like I had seen in the mob movies, I kept my mouth shut during questioning.

What plants?

Coincidentally this happened on the same day that I had been expelled from my high school for fighting and for attempting to run a business within the school.

Stealing had been so lucrative for me, that I carried this new skillset to my school. I stole protein bars (Because they were the most expensive small item) from the student store and then resold them outside by the lunch tables. As a bonus, they were often my favorite flavor so I could snack on any of my surplus inventory—win-win.

It had been going smoothly until one day the priest who oversaw the store (Yes, he was actually a priest), came to my lunch table and accused me of stealing. He said the student who was working the cash register claimed he saw me stuff my pocket with candy bars.

I pretended to be appalled.

Me??

I got taken in for questioning. They searched my backpack, but luckily I had already sold the loot. So, they let me off the hook. I should have been happy to get off so easily. I should have laid low.

Instead, I went straight to the store to face off with my accuser. Well, it was more like face-to-chest. He was a 6'3 football player. I was 132 pounds. He probably had 70 pounds on me.

"Why did you snitch on me like a bitch!?" I stared him down as I shouted. (This was the part where you had to make them think you're crazy, remember?)

He lumbered forward from behind the cash register.

"I aint a bitch!" He yelled back and towered over me.

I didn't break my stare. Then a shove sent me crashing into the aluminum bench behind me.

I got up and walked up to him before exploding with punches.
I had to make good on my threats. Just like when I was a kid, I still felt these things needed to be dealt with swiftly and decisively.

I instantly decided that jabs wouldn't work. So instead, I swung wide and went for haymakers. My buddy, David, from the wrestling team had showed me to use this technique. He was only 103 pounds, but when he put on a pair of boxing gloves, he could beat the crap out of anybody on the whole team.

Now, I got to put it to use. I connected a couple hard blows to the cheekbones that I was proud of, given that it was quite a reach for me.

Then, I made the mistake of trying to do a double leg takedown---with my backpack on. With his bearish weight, and my backpack holding me back, we hit a stalemate just as people rushed in to break up the fight.

For me, it was a hell of a time. I enjoyed the fight. The rush of it. The fun of trying to defeat your opponent. People began to cheer.

Seeing, that my opponent was angry, I said, "Hey man good fight." And tried to give him a hug. He was fuming. And I couldn't understand why. As far as I was concerned, we both gave our best and we could shake hands and walk away after words. Just like a wrestling match.

As fun as it was, that fight immediately got me expelled from school.

I was at an all-time low.

After some pleading, my parent's found a way to enroll me in a school in a neighboring city.

It was the middle of junior year. I knew no one and wasn't really interested in making friends.

But then, as I strolled in late to Mr. Knox's English class, I spotted a girl. She was gorgeous. She was wholesome. In class, I learned her name was Teresa. And I heard whispered behind me that she thought I was cute.

She was different than me. I was restless. While she radiated warmth and peace.

When our eyes met, I saw something I had never seen before. I instantly felt…at peace. She was laughing with her friends. Looking into her big brown eyes, I felt like I had known her for a lifetime.

I knew I needed to ask her out on a date. Because, I thought, if only she got to know me, we would fall in love.

Of course, I tried some of the usual pick-up lines. But they didn't work.

She saw through me, and warned me that she "can't date anyone who does shady things."

Who me?

She knew I was a bit different. And maybe not right for her. And although she continued to deny my requests to take her out on a date, she still walked over to talk to me with suspicious regularity.

I kept stopping by her desk to say "Hi" and ask her to let me take her on a date.

Until, on a summer night in July, she finally let me take her to the movies. We watched Harry Potter. And before dropping her off at home, we shared our first kiss.

At that point I dropped everything. I quit wrestling. I quit the childish stunts. And I spent all of my time with Teresa.

Maybe it was due to my new relationship with Teresa. Maybe it was the heartbreak I saw in my mother's eyes when the sheriff interrogated me. Whatever the reason, by this time I had decided to thoroughly clean up my act.

That year, some people had broken into my parent's new dental office and stolen a lot of their hard-earned things. I felt what it was like to be on the other end of theft. And I decided that I would succeed, not by tricking anyone, but by creating something that people loved.

Theft was cowardly. But building value, building something that people loved, now *that* was a worthy pursuit.

Teresa and I stayed in love even as we went on to college.

I saw college as an opportunity for a fresh start. There were no assholes in college—just people trying to learn.

It was around this time that my mom, always trying to keep her Ivancito on the right path, gifted me a book that was profoundly influential on me. It was "Freakonomics" by Steven Levitt.

This gem was exactly what I needed. It unraveled the secret power that governs our society—Economics. It explained the laws of economics using wild examples such as how sumo wrestlers decide to cheat and why most drug dealers still live with their moms. He explained how incentives rule the world and how we take environmental cues to decide how to behave.

Fired up about this new discipline that seemed to explain everything, I chose to major in Economics.

I specifically honed in on economic history and on Latin American revolutions because it reminded me of what my grandfather used to teach me as a young boy. When he would enter the room, he'd turn off my tv show, take out a pen and blank sheet of paper from his pocket, and illustrate a lesson.

He would explain the history of the world and the principles of logic, mathematics, and economics.

I treasured this man's advice like it was wisdom scrawled on an ancient scroll.

He taught me about how the Spanish Conquistadores ravaged South America and killed the off the Incas to take their gold. He recounted how the region eventually won back its freedom through revolutionary freedom fighters. An economist by training, he thought there were lessons to learn in these stories. Lessons of good and evil. He taught me of capitalism from the readings of Adam Smith and communism from Karl Marx.

So, in college, I continued where he left off. I learned how oppressive regimes persisted in South America. How large multinational corporations savagely exploited the working class. In modern day, many of these companies have been charged with crimes against humanity. But throughout the 1900's big powerful companies destroyed lives in order to reap massive profits. And this is what sparked a series of revolutions all across Latin America. Notably in Cuba through the communist revolutionaries, Che Guevara and Fidel Castro.

These revolutions caused chaos. Bloodshed. And it is the reason that my family left Peru when I was two years old.

I learned the deep impact that economics has. While business and economics can be used to improve people's lives, it can also create oppressive systems that yield massive profits to some but horrendous consequences for others.

As I studied, the story moved me. I fell in love with the theme of right versus wrong. The boy in me was reminded of Star Wars. The rebels versus the dark side.

And as much as my teenage shenanigans might have shown otherwise, the Christian in me saw a potential way to have a positive impact on the world.

This realization became deeply engrained within me ever since, just as engrained as the ethos that was passed on from my dad: *Don't be lazy.*

I did continue my hustles—but this time they were legitimate ideas to create value and turn that into a business. By the time I graduated college, I must have tried over 30 failed ventures. And Teresa was by my side for each and every one.

But my great idea still eluded me.

I thought maybe I should continue on to more schooling. getting a Masters in Economics.

But my grandfather convinced me that I should go to dental school to build upon the foundation my parent's had laid. He said everyone should learn history and economics, but to build a business, I needed a deep technical skill. He suggested that I could build my great business endeavor in the dental field.

So, I went beast-mode and got to studying. Within a year or so, I crammed through my pre-requisites, applied, and got in.

Immediately after finding out I had been accepted to dental school, I whisked Teresa off to Napa. After a hot air balloon ride over the valley, I serenaded her in front a small group of friends and family and asked her to marry me. Despite her best instincts, she said, "Yes!!"

I had waited until after I was accepted to dental school in order to apply because, I needed to show that I could provide financially.

We had a little acceptance party at my house in which my aunt Gloria made a tooth-shaped cake.

I asked my dad if he was proud.

He didn't look pleased.

He replied, "I'm not surprised you got in. Look at how much support you have. Remember, you're supposed to accomplish *more* than your parents."

I was wounded but I stayed quiet. Maybe because I agreed with what he said. That inside I knew that I was not yet worthy of praise.

Now in dental school, in was tooth-deep in biochemistry, pharmacology, dental anatomy. I was drowning in class II test cases, perio charting, and struggling to get my clinical notes approved.

The degree to which I became familiar with all things related to teeth became mind numbing. I started having dreams about the outlines of cavity preparations. My world became teeth…and binge drinking with friends on the weekends.

And for the life of me, I could not fathom what relevance this had toward building my business. Yet it was eating away all of my time…and the clock was ticking. I was twenty five and felt like I hadn't accomplished anything I could be proud of.

Or that my dad would be proud of.

You're supposed to accomplish more than your parents.

I thought to myself. Even if I complete all of this work in dental school. It is still not enough.
I panicked.

In moments of pressure, my instinct is to scramble. I often think back to high school wrestling. There are moments in competition, where neither wrestler has the upper hand, where they are both exposed and need to quickly find the dominant positioning. So you scramble like hell. Risking yourself momentarily, in order to gain the larger competitive advantage. I always loved that part.

And now, I thought it was time to scramble.

"That's why I have to drop out babe. This just isn't the way."
I explained to Teresa on the phone.

I felt so stupid and irresponsible. I felt like an idiot for insisting on "pursuing my dream" to build something great.

We proceeded to have one of those long, you-better-get-your-shit-together type of discussions that couples have.

Then, after midnight, fueled by frustration and several bottles of Red Stripe from my fridge, I scribbled all the possibilities on my whiteboard in the kitchen. I wrote out all of the things that I enjoyed in dentistry. Implantology was one of the main things--it was...the *only* thing.

So, I decided I would have to double down. After graduation, I could not stay a general dentist. I would have to pursue one of the specialties that allows you to be an authority on implants.

Those were either oral surgery, periodontics, or prosthodontics.

I crossed off oral surgery because it was common knowledge that you had to be top of the class to be accepted into one of those programs. I crossed of periodontics because the lectures I had attended about the myriad ways to measure the gums always made me slam my forehead into my keyboard.

So, the only choice was prosthodontics.

For inspiration, I Googled some leaders in the prosthodontics field. I found Misch, who was the most successful implant educator of his time. But it didn't fully resonate with me. So I continued searching…

Then I found The CEO.

The CEO was a phenom. He had blazed his own trail. He had founded implant companies and had them acquired by industry giants. The most recent was one of the biggest and most well known players in the industry!

He rode a Harley, he flew a plane, had a beach house, and lived life on his own terms. He did things his own way.

This was the level of badassery I could get on board with.

Surely, this would be worthy. Not only would my dad be proud of me, but maybe I could be proud of myself…

So, I decided, this was it.

I decided that one day, I would build an implant company and it will be worthy of this elusive approval that I sought.

I decided that I was going to be an implant badass like The CEO.

CHAPTER 2

So I decided to basically ignore all my school requirements. I'd no longer try to get any perfect test cases for fillings, no more worrying about perio requirements, none of that stuff. That was officially off of my radar. I just didn't have time for it. And I figured that by cramming and putting effort in when in really mattered, that I would graduate.

Passing and graduating was just expected—nothing special. After all, that's what my dad had said. Graduating is just expected. But succeeding, succeeding my way, that was the goal. And it was non-negotiable.

My mission was simple, hone the skills that got me to become an implant industry badass.

Learn business, learn implants. Period.

So, although they fulfilled no official school requirements, I took on droves of implant cases.

When it came to biochemistry and pharmacology, I just stared at powerpoints, memorizing the keywords, and high-yield concepts for the exam.

But for implants, I actually found textbooks online and got absorbed into them.

I studied the surgical techniques to the point where I could imagine doing the entire procedure, even though I had never drilled into bone in my life. I even studied emerging research topics in implants such as tissue engineering and 3D fabrication methodologies. I researched old patents and made my own drawings to try to improve upon the designs.

When my classmates saw me reading an implant textbook in class, they looked at me in disbelief.

"Why are you studying implants? Don't you know they aren't part of the requirements?", they asked.

My peers in dental school were incredibly intelligent. In undergrad it seemed like the average student didn't excel because they weren't dedicated enough. But now in dental school, everyone studied and everyone was smart. I felt like a total idiot. But I didn't care about competing for the best grade in Biochemistry or Physiology, or anything else for that matter. I didn't see how it could translate to becoming an implant badass.

So again, I often felt disconnected. Somehow apart. I've never been an extrovert. So, actually the person who socialized with my class on my behalf was Teresa. Although she was attending dental hygiene school 90 miles away in Stockton, it felt like *she* was the one in dental school and I was just the guy she brought along. The guy who sometimes attended class. The guy with the weird obsessions and eccentricities.

Teresa had this way about her that attracted people. She was always the person you wanted to talk to about your day. The person you wanted to go to happy hour with. The person you felt you could trust with anything.

We did party *a lot* with our group of friends, and I look back on those days with so much fondness. But over time, I stopped hanging out so much and I began to get quietly focused on my mission. Implant Badassery.

Sometimes, I just got up and walked straight out of class because I was bored to tears and felt I couldn't waste my limited time. Instead, I would wander around school, taking the elevator to the floors that nobody visited.

I would walk around the empty hallways, glancing into door windows, visiting empty classrooms, and browsing old bookshelves. It reminded me of what my dad used to do. Whenever something was interesting to him, an office space for lease or business for sale, he would go and peer through the windows and test the door handle. He was always weirdly curious about stuff and would just go in and start talking to people.

That was me on the 4th floor of the old UOP building. I looked around, peered through windows, tested door handles.

I believed that there was value out there that was going untapped. And as a result I met some wonderful people.

First, I met a scientist, Dr. Miroslav Tolar. He had an overgrown white beard that reminded me of a wizard, and actually, he did have that knowing twinkle in his eye of Dumbledore. His office had a plaque that read "Tissue Engineering Lab." From regular visits to see Dr. Tolar I learned about how tissue engineering might be able to build scaffolding that can help regenerate bone and even teeth. My mind raced with the applications for implantology.

Then, I met a very unlikely mentor, Dr. Gary Richards, a paleontologist who happened to work within the dental school. My only interaction with him had been watching him give an anatomy lecture, but from peering into his office I could see that there was much more to learn from this man. He was manipulating a 3d model of a skull on his computer. I knocked on his door and just plain asked what he was up to.

Like Dr. Tolar, Dr. Richards was clearly brilliant but he also had this sort of anti-establishment vibe. I got that from the way that he spoke, from his tattoos, and to the motorcycle he rode to the school every day. Also from the fact that he didn't care that I was skipping class to hang out with him. When talking about his research, he spoke in an excited way that didn't slow down to let you catch up with all the deep technical knowledge.

He showed me how to use computer gaming software to create 3D models from slices of radiographs. It took many visits (and skipped classes), but eventually I was able to use what I had learned to create a custom 3D printed implant and it won the 3rd year research competition.

I also wandered one additional floor up, to the executive offices, where I would often visit another valued mentor, Dr. Craig Yarborough. Dr. Yarborough would help me think about the tough questions of how to reconcile my desire for becoming a business leader, while being deep in the trenches of dental school exams, boards, and patients. With his guidance, I entered a business plan competition at the main campus's MBA program and our work won first place! And when I was getting ahead of myself, he and the dean of education, Dr. Nadershahi, steered me back to focus on not failing out of dental school.

And as I got dangerously close to failing, my two best friends in school, Dianna and Seewan, helped me study and get back on track. Although, I'm sure their association with me was detrimental to their own grades. One time instead of studying for our Pediatric Dentistry final, I convinced Seewan to watch Superbad and then to teach me how to juggle.

Back in clinic I was amassing a formidable pile of implant patients. I would have to study on my own to learn how to complete the cases. And on Monday nights, I would stay to watch a special show. On these nights, those students who dared take on an implant case had to stand up on stage and pitch their treatment plan to a panel of giants. To me, the men on the panel were like superstar athletes. Sadowsky, Nattestad, Bedrossian, and Gonzalez. These were the implant specialists. They wrote the books and articles, on this stuff. They knew everything. And everyone would crumble under the pressure of presenting to them.

Everyone—that is—except me.

This was like dinner-and-movie night for me. I would grab a sandwich, sit in the back row and watch people sweat. By going to all of these, I knew the questions they would ask, and I had no fear. My proudest moment was during questioning from Dr. Bedrossian, who was notoriously the most ruthless critic, not because he was mean, but because he was so experienced, and so blunt, that he could not take anybody's BS. It was after I had finished my presentation and anticipated all of Dr. B's questions, that he said "This is what

I would expect from a graduate prosthodontics level presentation. Well done, Ivan." That was affirmation that I was on the right track to becoming that implant badass.

The CEO would have been proud. Maybe my dad would have been impressed too.

Self-assured in my basic implant know-how, I sent out class-wide emails offering to help tutor people for their implant cases and exams. People started calling me "Implant Ivan."

While I nearly failed out of school because of the sparse attention to my requirements, I did make it to graduation day.

And what made that day more special was that I would walk the graduation stage with Teresa—who was graduating from the hygiene program. She had the hope that we would now settle down and start a practice together.

But by now she realized that I wanted to push on and learn all I could about implants. That I wanted to pursue a 3-year residency in prosthodontics.

But there was a problem. There was no way in hell that any prosthodontics residency would accept me. I simply didn't have the grades for it.

So, I turned to my prosthodontics instructors to help guide me.

Their response: *No way.*

They all said that I had no chance of getting in.

Instead, they suggested I do a 1 year of a general practice residency in order to qualify for a prosthodontics program.

But that was one whole year of doing stuff I had no interest in. One whole year of wasted time.

My dad's words would often play back to me:

Time is the most valuable thing you have. Don' t waste it.

I knew better than to close a door on myself. If the system won't accept you, you should try to bypass that system.

People use systems to make life manageable, but at the end, it is still humans who make the ultimate decision. My applications had been filtered to the "reject" pile. I knew that because a month had gone by since I submitted my application. So instead, I sought to make the human connection.

University of Michigan was my top choice residency because they said that residents get to place as many implants as they want! So, I bought a ticket to Michigan.

As I walked from the bus stop to the brick dental school building, my knees ached from the frigid Midwest breeze. But I managed to give the best damn showing of myself and my implant knowhow. They gave me an interview on the spot and 2 weeks later, they offered me a spot in the residency.

Back in California, I wrestled with the decision.

I felt like I was seeing the word "Michigan" everywhere—on tv and in magazines.

One day, on a family vacation, I went on a walk with my mom.

"I think I'm seeing signs everywhere that are steering me towards Michigan!" I told her.

She stopped walking, looked at me and said, "There are no signs, hijo. You just have to pray about it."

Then suddenly, my eyes widened as they caught a glimpse of something behind my mom.

"MOM LOOK!!!" I shouted and pointed behind her.

There was literally a street sign glued up on a wall. It read "Michigan St." We both erupted in laughter before she replied, "I guess you're going to Michigan!!"

So I decided it was time to make my pilgrimage to Michigan for the next part of my "implant badass" training.

But first, I had to convince Teresa to go through with marrying me.

Teresa came from a conservative Vietnamese family. They grew up on, 'Go to church, stay safe, fly under the radar, and be stable.' Her parents were hard working immigrants like mine. They worked at the same jobs for 20 years. Day in day out, same hard hours.

Above all else, they valued, stability.

Teresa asked me, "We were supposed to move back home. But now we're moving across the country. If we move there, how will we be...stable? Will we have stability?"

I sounded out that word, enunciating every syllable as if learning it for the first time.

Sta-bi-li-teeee.

Teresa's parent's trusted that I was going to graduate, pay the bills, and take care of their daughter.

But this talk of dropping out? Talk of dreams? This was different.

It was *instability*.

Her dad was a man of few words. When something was not to his liking, he simply labeled it "No good."

And instability was 'no good' indeed.

"Are you sure we should get married...*right now*?", Teresa asked me.

I knew I had to do it right away.

And I had to act fast.

Deep down I didn't know what the hell I was doing. I knew that we wouldn't be stable for a long while. But I also knew, to my core, that I would be successful. That I would make it happen.

So I made her the promise she needed to hear. The promise that I had to believe too. That I would bring us stah-bi-li-teee. That I would get with the program and help us live a peaceful, settled life. Go big or go home.

Our wedding was the biggest party I had ever attended. We exchanged vows and partied like we had never partied before. We had overestimated how much alcohol we needed for our open bar. So, everyone got hammered and we all ended up in the pool in tuxedos and dresses at midnight including my little brother and sister. A couple broke up at the wedding. Someone got punched in the head. Someone passed out with their legs hanging outside of their car in the parking lot. My grandfather disapproved of it all. But it was a magnificent blur. One hell of a party.

But before the party, at the ceremony I promised Teresa that after I graduate as a prosthodonist, we would move back to our hometown of Stockton, and we would be stable. Home in the suburbs and Home Depot on the weekends. We would have our safe nest to raise our kids and cherish our time with them.

I reassured her over and over, that I would make more than enough money take care of my student loans. After all, my dad had said that prosthodontists make $400,000 right out of school, so of course we would be stable.

I would be well on my way to building a successful implant business and becoming an implant badass like The CEO.

A week before we embarked on our journey to Michigan, my dad pulled out an old box full of implants and models of jaws. He slid over an old sawdust model of a mandible and handed me an implant. It was an old Nobel Replace. The ones with that trilobe connection that was rumored to have weak spots in the platform. But at the time, it was one of the most commonly used implant.

He said, "Place this one hundred times into these models. Try hard spots too. Don't make it easy for yourself."

Later that afternoon he called me into his operatory.

He told his patient in Spanish, "Mira amigo, mi hijo te va poner el implante. No te preocupes. Yo lo voy a supervisar."

He was reassuring his patient that I would be doing the implant, but that everything would be okay.

As I drilled, he pushed my untrained hand along the path it was supposed to follow. I clumsily maneuvered the drill as it jumped around and the patient's mouth was quickly filling up with blood and saliva. I tried not to show my nervousness. I was known as 'Implant Ivan' by some students at school but I had never actually placed an implant.

I had better not mess up now.

My hand shook a bit more, as I lowered the slowly spinning implant into the little pool of blood that awaited it inside of the hole I had just created. Its roughened matte surface was pristine, just before becoming enveloped in blood. As I cranked the steel wrench, I watched the implant slowly sink deeper until it lay perfectly encased within the bone with which it would fuse.

The fusion between titanium and human bone would begin now. Over the course of the next 3 months, the body's cells would deposit bone right onto the implant surface. I had initiated it. I *made* this happen.

I felt a sense of power and wonder. Marveling at the ability I now possessed to induce this biological phenomenon.

And then it was done. I was officially an implant placer. I did many more that week with my dad. Each with its little mistakes. But gradually improving.

With my newly acquired skill and my newly acquired wife, we parted with our families, hopped in our white Subaru Outback and made the cross-country drive to Ann Arbor, Michigan.

CHAPTER 3

Prosthodontics training was not what I expected.

Everyone had told me that Michigan would be transformational. Dr. Tolar, the bioengineering wizard, had called it "The Mecca!"

So, I arrived excited to start placing implants, start doing research, and other crazy cool stuff. I was so enthusiastic about continuing my 3D printing dental implants research, but I didn't find my supervisors as enthusiastic about it. Instead, I spent so many hours reading dental literature and making dentures, that I wanted to stab myself in the eye with a high vac suction tip. The reading was nonstop and it was ancient.

Things were not going at my pace. I was impatient. I wanted to be placing implants already. I wanted to learn to graft. I wanted to do research!

But I didn't find those opportunities in my first year at Michigan.

So, frustrated, I decided maybe I had chosen the wrong program. Again, I thought of quitting.

So, one night, I turned to Teresa with the bad news. "Hun, I think I made a mistake. Maybe I should drop out and apply elsewhere. Maybe I should try to get into an oral surgery program."

She was quiet.

I continued, "I don't think this is where I can become the best I can be."

She let out a frustrated groan. "You got in despite your grades being awful. Why can't you just be happy?"

Then she asked, "Why do you have to be *the best*? Why is that so important?"

I didn't know how to answer.

It is in my genetic makeup. Some defect in a neural pathway.

I am incapable of not trying to be the absolute best. To *build* the absolute best.

It's a motor in my mind that is constantly whirring. Restless. Nonstop. And if something gets in the way, it triggers anger.

An addiction? A dysfunction?

It runs in some of the men in my family.

I'm convinced we all have some diagnosis. But the Chicchon men would never resort to getting tested for that kind of stuff.

Instead, we live with it. A drive to irrationally persist at all costs. You can find that in my dad. You could find it in my grandfather, who was still planning massive projects in his eighties.

And Teresa was just learning this about the man she married. As she was starting to put the pieces together, she realized that this was what she could expect for the rest of her life.

All she wanted was to settle down and start a family. She wanted children. That was her dream.

She was expecting a husband who would just work a normal job and spend time with his family. Instead, here I was dragging her across the country, stacking up a massive student debt burden, and making her question when we would be stable enough to have kids.

While I was busy complaining, *she* was the one who was working hard to provide for us. Since arriving at Michigan, Teresa had immediately found a job as a dental assistant and was working towards getting her hygiene license approved. She would go to work every day, and cook and clean, and then have to put up with my nonsense.

Looking back, I wouldn't have blamed her for leaving me and finding someone who was "more normal" or who wanted a more "normal" life.

We had many hard nights debating this.

But in the end, thankfully, Teresa's level-headed reasoning won me over.

"Finish what you started, and we'll figure it out," she decided.

I reluctantly agreed.

So, like back in dental school I forced that experience to become what I needed. I devoured implant wisdom from anywhere I could. I was a prosthodontics resident, but you could just as likely find me in the Periodontics department shadowing a sinus lift, or in the university hospital OR assisting for a jaw reconstruction.

I didn't actually have access to the hospital, so I would wait outside the staff entry doors at 6AM, for someone to come by and swipe their card. As they walked in, I would quickly slip in behind them. I would find where the oral surgery team was and would go hang out with them. Eventually they let me scrub in and do some small things to assist them. Usually it consisted of holding retractors, suctioning, and sometimes stitching. But I got a lot of experience just by being there.

University of Michigan oral surgery was truly a thing to behold—and I had a front row seat. It was a big cancer program. Hospital lore had it that their program director, Sean Edwards, was a certified genius. That, even though he came from a dental background, his medical board examination results were higher than anybody had ever seen—dentists or medical doctors alike.

He was a big man. Tall with a hockey players build. When he approached patients and picked up his scalpel, he relaxed into a slightly leaned posture. It was the surgeon's stance and it was evident that he could hold that stance for 12 hours or more if needed—as he often did.

After a 6-year oral and maxillofacial surgery residency, he had completed dual fellowships in microvascular surgery and pediatric craniofacial surgery. And he spoke in a fast, quiet, mumble, that could recall any surgical technique or the literature-based evidence that supported it.

I had the honor of assisting him several times. And each time was one of the greatest moments of my academic career. One time he worked on a young boy who was flown in from Haiti.

The boy was born with a facial deformity which completely obliterated his jaw.

Edwards made an incision at the ribcage. He stuck a saw inside, and proceeded to saw off of the boys ribs. Then pulled it out and cut and carved until it resembled half of a jaw along with the joint that the bone fits onto (called the TMJ).

It was then that I truly fell in love with surgery. And I hoped that I could earn my rank among such men.

Around that same time, you could also find me in the medical school collaborating on a book publication in head and neck anatomy. After working on my book contributions, I stayed late into the night practicing surgical techniques on the cadavers by myself in the anatomy lab. In the empty anatomy lab, I honed my surgical skills.

I also spent an ungodly amount of time in the engineering lab learning to use software to fabricate novel devices—building on the skills I gained from working with Dr. Richards. I developed a special technique that would be used in surgery and I got this technique published in the International Journal of Prosthodontics.

I was also lucky to gain pearls of wisdom from some of my mentors within the Prosthodontics program itself.

Although I resented the amount of reading that was forced upon us, Dr. Charlie Beard implanted into our brans the ability to read volumes of literature and extract useful interpretations. I would often wake up at 4AM to power through all the literature before our 8AM meetings in the frigid basement of the school

Dr. Jeff Rodney, with his nervous energy and obvious obsession with prosthodontics killed us by never approving any of our work. Every single 3-hour appointment he oversaw became a re-appointment. But it was because he wanted to teach us the absolute highest level of mastery. Prosthodontic perfection.

Then there was our maxillofacial prosthodontics instructor who resembled a wrestling coach. He was all smiles outside of class. But in class, he taught from the textbook that he had written himself and if you got anything wrong, you were in trouble. Whether the information was "in the reading" or not, Dr. Marunick would hold you responsible for knowing EVERYTHING.

"You call yourself a *doctor*?" He would peer into your soul. "Then why don't you know the answer??"

He taught me to take my profession and myself seriously. It was a sacred skill were learning and using to rehabilitate our patients.

My program director, Michael Razzoog, taught me one of the most valuable lessons of all. He told me the most important thing I should be doing during my residency is spending time with my wife which was advice I should have taken to heart.

In my second year at Michigan, I found out that one of the first-year residents, Andy Dill, was running a dental practice on the side. So, I bought $10,000 worth of Nobel Active implants, surgical kit, and a motor, and asked Andy if he would rent his practice to me whenever I could find patients. I'd pay him 10% of the production. He agreed.

Teresa and I made fliers that said "$999 Implants" and handed them out all over town. We left stacks at Mexican meat markets and also left them on windshields despite people yelling at me for putting junk on their car. Some lady, enraged that we put the flier on her windshield, yelled, "Whatever they're payin ya, it's not worth it!!"

We took care of everything ourselves. I would schedule patients from my cell phone and Teresa would take payments. Then, we'd scrub in and I'd do the surgeries as she assisted. By then she had also gotten her Michigan license for hygiene by then, so we worked hard to line up deep cleaning patients for her. As cool as I thought implants were, it was Teresa's deep cleaning treatments that truly helped pay the rent!

One day I brought in a patient for extractions. I extracted the first 3 teeth in 10 minutes. The last tooth took me 3 hours.

Another time, I was impatient because Teresa was applying the whitening gel very slowly and meticulously on the patient's teeth. I imagined what my dad would do. So, I asked to jump in and I did it FAST. So fast that I accidentally spilled the whitening gel on the patient's neck. He started itching uncontrollably and couldn't continue. It was a total fiasco.

Then we noticed a drop had fallen on Teresa's leg. It had burned a hole in her pants.

I also drove office-to-office, asking doctors if they were interested in having a part-time implant placer in their practice. Everyone rejected me.

By this time, aside from hustling to get patients at Andy's office, Teresa was working as a hygienist at two other offices. We discovered that the sure-fire way for me to get an implant gig was for Teresa to get a job first, and then to recommend me as an implant placer later.

So, that's how she got me a job at Dr. R's office where I would roll in with a box of equipment two times per month and place implants.

The office was located inside of an old-style home. As I rolled in with my box full of scalpels and implants, I couldn't help but feel like one of those old-school barber surgeons that made house calls.

Things had also finally picked up within my prosthodontics program. Whereas in dental school I had seeking out implant cases, in residency I sought out implant complications. My workbench was always the messiest—stacked with big implant cases only. I tried to avoid doing anything else.

I was also making monthly visits to California to have high-production implant marathons at my parent's office.

My life became implants and surgery.

And so it was then that I started noticing some flaws in the systems.

One of my dad's biggest frustrations was that drills kept going missing. Each system had a lot of drills, but he now had multiple kits in his office —each with different drills that all looked very similar to each other. And no matter how much he tried, he just couldn't get his team to put everything back where it belonged.

You could be mid-surgery, and ready for your next drill and find that it was missing! Or even worse it would sometimes be the wrong drill!

Another frustration is that all of the kits were too big to fit properly into the sterilization machine. So you could only sterilize one kit at a time. Se we were constantly waiting for kits to finish sterilizing.

Aside from helping me hone my skills, flying to California each month for these surgery marathon helped me to understand the shortcomings of various systems. That's when I started to truly feel the need for a better implant system.

Back in Michigan over lunch at the hospital, one of the oral surgery residents told me, "If you did an oral surgery residency after prosthodontics, you'd be a total Implant Ninja!"

It was a tempting idea and I had been giving it thought.

I stayed up many late nights wrestling with the idea of continuing on to a six-year oral surgery program after my 3-year prosthodontics residency was over. I even made the mistake of bringing the idea up to Teresa. She ultimately said that she would not stop me, but that she didn't support the idea at all. And that it was, without a doubt, the wrong thing for our marriage and future family.

"You're not going to move me across the country, away from my family, and want us to have children but NOT BE THERE FOR THEM!", she shot back.

In the end, I didn't pursue oral surgery. But the name "Implant Ninja" stuck.

I started my Implant Ninja YouTube channel, and then I made an Implant Ninja blog to share what I was learning.

I milked every ounce of experience I could possibly gain out of my time in Michigan. Except for when it came to what mattered most, my marriage. I had taken Teresa to a foreign place, and rather than having her new husband to enjoy it with, she had a husband who left early and came home late. When my program had a vacation, I would spend my time holed away in the engineering lab or in the operating room. She had many lonely meals accompanied only by our little white dog, Sophie. I wish I could go back in time to be her friend when she needed one most. I wish that I had understood that she needed me, more than I needed to learn. But I didn't.

We did have some fun times. But we also had some exceptionally low moments—where we even discussed divorce.

During one particularly low moment, I privately confided in my mom,

"Mom, I really messed up. I think Teresa's gonna leave me…"

Next thing I knew, Teresa got a call from both of her parents. Her mom and dad reminded her of what a wonderful partner I was.

My mom called Teresa too. She said she understood how hard-headed I could be. She apologized on my behalf.

Later my mom would tell me that she had driven straight over to Teresa's parents house to hatch a plan to keep us together.

So by luck, and a bit of conspiracy, Teresa was still married to me when I walked the stage of my graduation ceremony after 3 years of prosthodontics training.

And now we were ready to drive back home where I would earn $400k per year, start building my business, and find this long-awaited *stability*.

And what made the trip back home even more special, is that after two years of trying to conceive, we were coming home with a little baby in Teresa's womb.

CHAPTER 4

We were back home in the central valley of California, and I was walking on clouds. I had finally accomplished something both of my parents were proud of. They couldn't stop telling people that their son was a Prosthodontist!

I had graduated with a dental specialty certificate. I was married to my high school sweetheart. I was about to start making real money. And I had a daughter on the way.

I finally allowed myself to indulge in feeling "successful."

Then, a few days after making the drive back from Michigan, I got an email from 'MyFedLoans.gov.' The email plainly informed me that starting the following week they would start withdrawing $8,300 from my checking account… EVERY MONTH.

And that it would continue that for 10 years.

My chest tightened a bit. I didn't own a house yet but my $800,000 student loan debt sure felt like a mortgage.

No worries, I guess I have to earn a bit more money than I expected, and I had better earn it fast.

I confidently sauntered over to the computer, interlaced my fingers and cracked my knuckles. I typed, "prosthodontist jobs" in the search bar. I was ready to start swimming in my $400k per year salary.

But what I saw on the screen, left me utterly confused.

Only 2 search results in the whole state. And they paid LESS than a general dentist salary!

Ho Li Shit.

How the hell could that be?

I didn't have time to figure it out right then. I had to accompany Teresa to a doctor's appointment, so I closed the window, put on a confident grin and hopped into my trusty Subaru.

At her regular 3-month visit, her obstetrician had referred us to a specialist because she had spotted something..."irregular."

Now, sitting down with the specialist, Teresa and I nervously held hands and listened to what he had to say.

As soon as he started talking, it all became a blur. As he spoke, his lips moved in slow motion and his voice became distorted.

The words I could make out were "TERATOMA" and "TERMINATION OPTIONS."

Then, with a chipper demeaner he parted with, "so think it over and next time we'll discuss termination options." On the drive home, I replayed it in my mind. I hoped that somehow I had misunderstood. But, as the truth settled, I sat stunned and helpless.

Teresa sat quietly behind the wheel, with a steady drip of tears puddling on her maternity dress.

Her dream, crushed.

Instability.

All she had wanted was to settle down and start a family. And now it was being taken away.

There must be another way, I thought. So, I switched from stunned confusion to manic determination.

There had to be a way to make this right.

Suddenly, the money I owed seemed meaningless. Money meant nothing. Also, my goal to build something great suddenly felt…childish. My new fatherly primal instinct overcame me. I was determined to find a way to bring my daughter into the world and provide her the quality of life she deserved.

I felt anger, blind determination, and even hate. I clenched my teeth until it hurt—daring my enamel to shatter.

She will THRIVE. I told myself.

But...then a nauseating feeling crawled up from my heart to my throat. Regardless of the health of my daughter, regardless of anything I was going through,

I *had* to pay the money I owed.

Debtors don't give a shit. You pay or you...what...flee the country? Fake your death?

It was made clear to us in the last year of dental school. YOUR DEBT IS NOT FORGIVABLE.

As much as I wanted to not think about money, I needed to.

And if I wanted to get the best care for my daughter, I had to be ready to pay any amount needed for her medical care. There was no way around it.

But I was so broke. And my net worth was so negative.

My wife had asked for me to bring stability. And now we had medical instability and financial ruin.

Well, fuck you very much, life.

But, I was a family man now. And a man provides.

It runs deep in our genes, scrawled on cave walls by our ancestors-back when a caveman would go out into the treacherous unknown with a club to fend off predators for the sake of protecting his cavewoman and cave-kids.

As he dragged back a slab of T-Rex meat, I'm sure he grunted, "Stability...good."

Back then, all they needed was a cave, a fire, and some animal flesh. Life was supposed to be better now. But how I longed to be that caveman, who had never heard of federal student debt.

When we arrived home, I couldn't speak. My mom saw Teresa crying and came over to embrace her. As they stood there, it looked like Teresa might fall to the ground if my mom's arms weren't holding her up.

I walked into the house without a word. Then, I saw my brother, Danny, with a group of his friends walking through the house. Without a word, I lumbered towards him, and embraced him. As I squeezed him, I began to cry uncontrollably. In that moment, I had no words. But my brother's embrace was what I needed.

I composed myself enough to stumble back to the computer.

I had already frantically grasped for information about the medical condition on the drive home, and had reached out to my surgeon friends from Michigan. Depleted and discouraged from that search, I now brought up the tab that reminded me that I had no job prospects. Again, I desperately searched for jobs. But my computer had no answers for me.

Again, I turned angry.

Hadn't I done all this schooling so that I could be successful? Hadn't I done what the world said I should? Why then, can't I even take care of my family?

At least the anger woke me up. I became driven by the cortisol and adrenaline in my veins.

I decided it was time for me to man the fuck up.

It was then that I made a promise to myself that I would keep my family safe and that I would never compromise on their health or safety because of my financial shortcoming.

I would provide. I would give my family the best. Just like my parents had done for us.

I would bring *stability*.

I just had to figure out how.

CHAPTER 5

After seeking second opinions, we found a team willing to take on our case. The high risk OBGYN at UCSF said that they could most likely deliver her safely at their hospital. They told us that it was in fact NOT a teratoma, as the previous doctor had called it.

It was a condition called a lymphatic malformation. And it was not inherently lethal.

But given that it was located on her face and neck, it was still potentially life threatening as it could swell up and prevent her from breathing.

The high-risk obstetrician said, "I have to tell you that there is a small possibility that we would have to use a highly advanced delivery method, called the EXIT procedure. But *we would only resort to it in a worst-case scenario.*"

And then she said, "there is also a small risk that we might lose the baby or the mom, but that is very unlikely."

I worried about this incessantly. The morbid thought lingered in my mind. The idea of losing the baby and losing Teresa was too much. It reminded me of one of my heroes, Theodore Roosevelt, who had lost his wife and his mom on the same day. I was reminded that people who overcome major challenges become infinitely stronger people as a result. But I didn't want to become stronger. I just wanted my family to be safe.

As I prepared for our hospital trip, I was rummaging through some cabinets to find a notebook that I could use as a journal for our stay. Any old blank notebook would do.

I came across a brown notebook that said this on its cover:

"Be still and know that I am God."

I felt this deep in my soul. I wished I could believe that everything would be alright, but I didn't.

Again, I cried.

Then, one day. Teresa started bleeding before her due date. So we drove to UCSF where they resorted to that worst-case-scenario option.

It took a large team of doctors who swapped in and out of the operating room. They cut Teresa open at the waistline, and they delivered our daughter's hand first...and started an IV line on it. Then, they delivered her head and intubated her immediately prior to cutting the umbilical cord.

I was holding Teresa's hand as she was waking up in the recovery room when a nurse told me that she could take me to see my daughter. Cold with nervousness, I quietly made my way through the neonatal intensive care unit. I found myself getting more excited and nervous as I got closer.

Outside of her room, a little glass plate mounted on the door read "Baby Girl Nguyen."

As soon as I entered, my heart sank. The nervousness turned into sadness. I stood, not moving, just watching my daughter. . She had just emerged from her MRI. She was entangled in a mess of cords and tubes. Her chest pumped mechanically with the help of a large tube taped into her mouth. The medical tape stretched from cheek to check further disfigured her face. On her head she wore a massive pair of yellow earmuffs. Her skin, a chalky red.

She didn't look peaceful. She looked like a wild creature from another planet who had been captured and taken to a laboratory.

She was finally here. And while she was safely brought into the world, hers was a different world than the one we live in. It was a world of tubes, and needles, and relentless beeping of machines.

We lived in the hospital with her for a month, during which we came to know a burden which we couldn't have imagined before we became parents. They told us our daughter was unstable. They said she needed immunosuppressant medication. She was poked and prodded constantly.

The glass plate outside her hospital room came to read, "Olivia," a name that Teresa gave her, which represents peace. We hoped that someday soon, she would find it.

We were discharged under the condition that we give Olivia an immunosuppressant that was supposed to help keep her malformation from spontaneously swelling and blocking her airway.

At that moment she was safe, but helping her thrive with a lymphatic malformation on her neck and face was the next challenge. It was a genetic mutation, that causes, among other things, for the lymphatic vessels to grow into little bubbles rather than as a continuous hose that drains the lymph fluid. So as the fluid is produced, and it has nowhere to go, and her little face and neck would swell. Her tongue and the floor of her mouth would fill up like a distended balloon.

When that happened, it was an emergency.

Teresa and I would have to drop whatever we were doing and speed to the hospital emergency department. I carried a tiny pink airway appliance in my pocket so that, if it ever came down to it, I could attempt to stabilize her airway while we waited for an ambulance.

Still, I had to find a way to pay the bills, specifically that $800k hanging over my head. On this quest, I went out to lunch with local lab technicians and picked their brains. In one of these lunch meetings, I sat eating spaghetti with a man who owned a fast-growing implant laboratory.

He told me he had a problem. One of his best clients was having trouble. He discreetly said that the dentist could "use some help." And he told me I should pay her a visit.

I made the 2.5-hour drive to this quaint little office in California wine country, leaving Teresa to take care of Olivia on her own for the day. The guilt of leaving them to work always made me work harder and put an immense pressure on me to be as productive as possible with my time.

At this implant center, I saw that there were huge implant cases being done on a daily basis. But when I saw the quality of the clinical work, I was dumbfounded. It was a total shitshow. Implant complications galore.

This was a godsend for someone like me! I had a lot of training in fixing implant complications during my residency. And now this opportunity had been waiting especially for me. I was so excited that I told the doctor I'd start right away.

Two days per week I made the 5-hour roundtrip commute up to wine country and place a ton of implants and troubleshoot a a ton of cases.

As it turns out, the doctor was going blind—so she had me take over her surgeries as well as her prosthetic work.

I was placing a lot of implants from Straumann and Nobel Biocare and Implant Direct and I was restoring some lesser known brands such as Thommen Implants and older models such as Brannemark and IMZ. More importantly I was managing complications for those systems so I got to see the extreme situations that you'd encounter with these implants. Fractured teeth, loose full sets of implanted teeth, stripped screws, and failed implants were things that I would regularly be asked to fix.

One of the biggest challenges I faced was that all the implants had a different platform designs, different sizes, and different screwheads. It seemed outrageous to me that implant companies would make it this difficult for the consumer.

The doctor had big tubs that contained random parts from each brand. You'd be lucky if you could ever find what you needed! It caused so much confusion that I started bringing in a collection of wrenches and bits in my backpack, and I would have that with me at all times. I was always ready to restore anything. If someone's implant tooth fell out at Starbucks, I was ready to screw it back in.

At first, the job was a godsend. It allowed me to make my student loan payments, I was back to placing titanium, and the complexity of the work gave me a mental break from the sadness and uncertainty surrounding my daughters condition.

But then, things started to feel off.

One day a patient jokingly said he would sue us. And then another said the same thing.

Another time, the doctor was doing the sedation for my full arch surgery, and in the middle of it I noticed her staring out of the window before shouting "OH SHIT ITS THE COPS!"

"What the hell is going on?" I asked myself as I continued drilling into the patient's jaw.

The police came in to question her and I was left alone in the middle of the surgery. The patient quickly started desaturating - or losing blood oxygen level -- after she left. I had to insert a plastic airway device in his mouth and pinch the crap out of his shoulders, and barking the order for him to, "BREATHE!!" (I had gotten used to dealing with these desaturation issues when that doctor was holding the reins for anesthesia)

Each day working there was mayhem. And sometimes I had the pleasure of being assisted by none other than my dad. He loved seeing the crazy cases that I was troubleshooting. Now *he* was the one going on ridealongs with *me*!

As usual my dad sensed the business opportunity. "Ivan, this place is a goldmine!" I started to believe it too.

Then, he assisted me on a case where I was placing 8 implants on a 350 pound native American man. Before the surgery, the man gave us the instructions:

"Strap me down, anesthesia doesn't work on me....seriously."

Reluctantly, my dad brought out his bright orange truck straps. We glanced at each other in bewilderment as we wrapped the Husky straps around this mans big body, locking him to the chair.

The owner doctor started the IV line. And I began cutting.

This man thrashed his massive head side to side as I cut and drilled and stitched. His roar reverberated throughout the empty office. Somehow, I placed 8 implants, in a record time.

As my dad spent more time there, his optimism began to fade.

The owner doctor had the habit of exploding in rage. In the middle of the surgery she would yell, "WHAT THE FUCK ARE YOU DOING!! WHER IS MY RETRACTOR!!!! ARE YOU AN IDIOT???"

If anything went wrong with a lab case, she would promptly pick up the phone and yell, "IM GOING TO FUCKING SUE YOU!!! WHY ARE YOU DOING THIS TO ME???"

She tried messing with me, but I didn't take shit from anyone. She only tried that once.

Needless to say, morning huddles were dismal. "WHAT THE FUCK HAPPENED TO MY PRODUCTION???" was a common theme for the morning.

When my dad caught a glimpse of one of her tirades, his optimism disappeared, and he warned me to be cautious.

Then, finally one day I heard "DR. IVAN COME QUICK!!!"

I ran in to the operatory next door and found a patient who was pale blue. As blue as the sky. Not moving. Lifeless.

I immediately shouted to the receptionist to call 911 and I started CPR. I cut their shirt off, started compressions, and shouted for the defibrillator.

The fire department arrived 5 minutes later.

When the fire fighters switched with me, I locked myself in the bathroom. I knew the patient was dead. Their blue face reminded me of a zombie from a movie. It felt unreal.

I thought of this person's family. Their children and grandchildren that would never see them again. In the darkness of the bathroom, I put my hands to my face and cried.

When I heard a knock on the door, I dried my face and stepped out.

They had resuscitated her. Amazingly, this person would live. She would live. But not without filing a major lawsuit.

I walked out and called Teresa to tell her what happened. We decided the best thing was to call my malpractice insurance right away and make sure my ass was covered. Apparently, I was on the hook for this as well and could potentially be sued because I was involved in the CPR.

The job had been an amazing training experience for me in so many ways. But there was too much stress that accompanied the work. Too much liability that I wanted no part of.

Someone from the California Dental Board, complete with a gun and badge, came out to question me about the incident. We met at a Panera bread. He put his badge on the table.

He interrogated me as he munched on his potato chips. My eyes kept drifting to his gun.

"Why would this man need a gun?", I wondered.

I worried about the patient suing me. I worried about the doctor retaliating against me for "snitching" on her. I recalled what I had done after the guy snitched on me back in high school. Then I proceeded to tell the interrogator everything.

After my interview, I feared that one day the doctor might show up at my home and stab me. Yes, I seriously thought this was a possibility. Some people just give you a stabby vibe. After all, it was just me and Teresa and Olivia at home. So I took care not to leave them at home by themselves for too long.

I was 29, but in between this stressful work environment and all the emergencies my daughter had, I decided "I'm too old for this stuff."

So, I quit my job. I took some time to be home and re-evaluate how I was going to keep making my student loan payments with a more manageable level of stress.

CHAPTER 6

Anyone who's had a baby knows the drill. As a new parent, you're basically a zombie. Half awake, you don't have the attention or energy to do much of anything.

All the uncertainty--my daughter's emergencies, the stress from that crazy dental office--had been constant injections of adrenaline. I needed something peaceful. I needed to get grounded.

So, I turned my attention back to the goal of creating something great. Back to my implant company.

I tried to form a legal entity, but when the request for my original name "Golden Coast Implants" was denied, I inexplicably chose the name Intrepid Llama LLC. You know it's bad when the person on the phone says, "Are you sure you want to name your company that?"

Yes, I seriously named it that. I envisioned this as an anonymous holding company with a unique name. But looking back, it seems like such a ridiculous name for a fledgling implant company.

As the new owner of Intrepid Llama, I dusted off my old implant notebook and drew up dental implant designs. I contracted a CAD designer and had schematics of my implant made. While Olivia napped, I found a machine shop that would fabricate samples for me. I sent them impression copings and torque wrenches and asked if they could make those for me as well. (As you can probably tell, I had a very primitive understanding of how this all worked.)

They shot me back their invoice: $10,000 to manufacture a sample of one implant. *Yikes.* I couldn't pay for that. So, I set that idea aside for the time being.

Needing to feel like I was making progress *somewhere,* I studied the FDA compliance process involved with starting an implant company. I sifted through droves of articles and legal documents. I spoke with a lawyer and found out that bringing an implant to market would cost me upwards of $100,000 in legal and compliance fees alone. So, I set that idea aside too.

The motivation was there, but I simply didn't have the money to start my implant business yet. On the contrary, I had just quit my job. And now despite my unstable schedule with all of my daughter's emergencies, I needed to find a way to pay the bills and then hopefully to get some start-up capital for my implant business.

Looking for motivation, I turned to books. As my hands were always tied up with carrying the baby, I downloaded 2 audio books that were profoundly influential: The Hundred Dollar Start up and The 4 Hour Workweek.

These books were a deep dive into a new way of doing business and new way of life. Reading them gave me hope.

I learned three big lessons from them:

One:

I needed to create cash flow before spending tons of money. Cash flow confirms that people want what you are selling.

Two:

My expertise was valuable to others and so I could create an informational product around it. And I didn't need to wait 30 years before I could teach.

Three:

I needed to focus on being effective versus being busy. By focusing on effectiveness, it was possible to earn a good income even with all of the instability in my schedule and life overall.

I thought, well shit, I learned a lot about full arch implant complications in residency. And I just went through a stressful real life boot camp in full arch implantology at this implant center. Why don't I make an ebook about that?

I started generating some interest by writing lengthy blog posts about the techniques I was using. These would serve as chapters for the future book. The website was garbage. It took me one night to throw it together. But to my surprise, people read it! AND THEY COMMENTED! WOOP!

It felt like I was on to something. It felt like this had potential.

So I called my dad and told him what I was up to.

He replied, "Why are you always trying to find a way to avoid working? If I was you, I would find a regular job and work six days a week."

Unfazed, I put my book up for presale before I had finished writing it. The next day, I saw that 30 people had pre-purchased it!

Now that I verified people were willing to pay for this, I got to the work of quickly writing the book as fast as possible.

I did nothing aside from watch the baby and write. I stopped shaving, stopped bathing, and stopped changing my clothes. I started looking (and smelling) like a homeless man inside my own apartment. Any time of the day, you could find me in a white robe, in my boxers, scruffy beard and a mug of coffee, hunched over at my computer or pacing around getting my thoughts straight.

I reached out to some people with implant-heavy Instagram accounts and asked if they wanted to contribute to the book. Dentists who I didn't know personally offered to contribute a considerable amount of case photos to what was becoming a substantial handbook!

I edited the entire thing which must have been around 300 pages, and then I threw together a quick cover for the book.

One of my physician friends scoffed, asking how I could expect to be taken seriously with a cover that "looks like a 5th grader made it."

But I felt like doctors were tired of reading stuffy textbooks. Technical and stuffy was the old way. Easy and actionable was the new way.

Then, on the morning that I put the book up for sale, I anxiously checked my email.

What I saw blew me away.

An entire email inbox full of "Order #101" "Order #102", Order #103…" etc filled the screen.

In my signature robe, I proudly walked over to where Teresa was feeding Olivia in the living room. I showed her the full inbox of sales.

Teresa yelled, BABE!! YOU DID IT!!!!! Now go shave and take a shower!"

While Olivia rolled around on her playmat, Teresa and I packed up books to send all over the world. $20,000 of sales came in that day. I would be able to make payments on my student loans for 2 more months.

CHAPTER 7

So, I had quit my job, but now my new handbook was selling like hotcakes and I was, once again, able to pay tuition, rent, and medical bills.

I also had started seeing some patients on my own. How?

About 2 years before graduation, I set up a website for my dental practice. I didn't actually have a dental practice yet, but I knew it would be helpful to start building the site before I actually needed it.

I filled it with as much useful and educational information possible for patients. By continually tweaking my site I was able to make it rank higher and higher on Google. So, by the time I had graduated, I already had patients calling my cell phone regularly for consultations.

This amounted to a small number cases at first. But by this time, I was getting more calls which were turning into a steady stream of full arch implant cases.

Taking on big cases was fun but working on the education side was more fulfilling for me. There was something more rewarding about connecting with my peers and helping them along their journey. So, I wanted to go deeper into it.

I drove out to my alma mater in San Francisco to meet with one of my old instructors. I told him about my experience and asked if maybe I could help as an instructor in one of their implant courses. He literally laughed at me.

"You? Haha! Maybe in 5 years or so. Go get some experience first."

Soon after, one of my friends from dental school told me, "Dude, you're trying to teach now? Don't you need more experience? Like, don't you need some grey hair?"

Instead of listening to them, I said, "Screw it, I'm donna do it on my own."

So, I posted up on my blog that I would be hosting courses myself! I invited docs to visit me in Stockton, California where I would coach them chairside as they did implant surgery on live patients.

Of course, my dad was always there. Watching from a distance, quietly worrying about what the heck his son was up to.

I had a lot of fun at these hands-on courses. I saw it as a way to hang out with some new friends and help them get started with surgery.

And it also helped that the people at Zimmer Biomet were supporting my courses. They would pay for lunch and help promote the event.

They were happy to do so because I had just spent $25,000 on switching to their implant system.
I had decided to switch over from Nobel Biocare because I was starting to notice some bone loss with the Nobel Active implants I had previously placed. At the time, I didn't know exactly why I was getting the bone loss, but I thought I would try another brand.

When the Zimmer rep first showed up at my office to introduce me to their system, I felt a bit overwhelmed by it. The surgical kit was big and seemed to contain a hundred little parts. I told him that I was a bit apprehensive about jumping into a new kit. But he assured me that he would be there to support me in whatever I needed.

"I'll be here for you doc" He told me with a wide, reassuring grin.

So I pulled the trigger.

I bought into the system and he came over personally to deliver it. But the day after selling me the kit, he requested a meeting with me. I thought it was for a nice get-to-know-you meeting.

It was not. He was quitting.

He introduced me to my new rep, Maggie. She told me "I'm new to dental, but I learn fast." Then after 2 months, she quit too.

With on again off again support from Zimmer, it was quite a bit of work to line up patients and continue hosting these classes. And I didn't like that my courses were only legal for California licensed dentists to participate. I wanted to build something that was accessible for everyone, not just California doctors.

So, in order to allow any licensed doctor to participate, I moved on to teaching on pig jaws.

On the morning of the teaching days, Teresa would drive our little white Subaru to a slew of Mexican meat markets in downtown Stockton to find pig heads. She would haul a big plastic container and show the bewildered butchers how to saw the heads so we could get as much bone surface as possible for the day's practice. As she hauled the payload and the bucket swished with pig juice, I imagine she was thinking *"this better be worth it."*

True to $100-dollar-start-up form, I hosted the courses out of my parent's living room. Most people appreciated it, but some doctors would get cold feet once they looked up the location on a map. They sometimes cancelled because they thought it was some kind of scam. As if I was trying to lure them to my home to kidnap them and hold them for ransom.

And truth be told, it was hard to fill seats because not everyone was willing to make the trip out to Stockton, California. It was far from the airport, there aren't that many flights, and it's not exactly a tourist destination. By this time, people had heard of Stockton's reputation. So, we were usually only able to get 10-15 people to attend each course.

I felt like much of my "audience" was excluded by the geographical limitation. Each time I put on a course, we spent so much time marketing and shouting from the rooftops "Come to my course!" It just didn't feel like a very effective way to build a business.

As I vented my frustrations about these limitations to Teresa, she cut me off blurted out, "Babe! You've got to do an online course!!"

CHAPTER 8

The year 2018 was a big one. After new MRI's and a scope, Olivia's ENT doctor, Dr. Meyer, told us her airway was much larger and more stable. And that there was no evidence of the malformation inside of her throat. Dr. Meyer said that she was finally able to confidently say that Olivia's airway was safe. I felt like *I* was the one who could breathe again.

Given Olivia's new medical stability, Teresa and I decided to open a dental practice. We found some space, converted it into a dental office, and started growing the hell out of it.

And, of course, we kept it *$100-start-up* style. We were able to build our office for $50,000 as opposed to the $500,000 that is more commonly seen with new dental start-ups. Nonetheless, our practice was a wonderful little dental home for us and our patients.

Teresa handled payments and customer service and I placed the implants. But unlike in our little moonlighting practice in Michigan, we needed some additional help.

My parent's had recently hired and trained one of my sister's classmates, Alvin Nguyen, as a dental assistant. He was a young guy looking for ways to gain experience. So, they suggested that he might find a good match with us.

Me, Teresa, and Alvin made that little $50,000 office look like a million bucks. I was proud to call it our own.

But perhaps we did too good of a job with marketing. Patients started pouring in. And not just simple cases. As I was basically the only prosthodontist (the other prostho in town didn't speak English), I got slammed with anybody who had any type of implant complication.

I loved the complexity of these cases. I felt like I was problem solving something interesting every day. I wanted to be the guy doing the big implant cases.

While my ego pushed me to do more complex stuff, Teresa warned me that I should probably stick to the easy implant cases. After all, we didn't need any more complexity in our lives. What we needed was a predictable business. But I didn't listen. I invited any and all implant cases my way. I wanted to earn my rank.

Soon enough I was drowning in "special cases." And we finally got busy enough to need to hire someone as a receptionist.

I learned that, while it might be a fun mental challenge to take on those cases, it doesn't work if you want to build a smoothly operating business.

Sure, it was profitable, but I started to come home later and later and grew more tired each day. I found myself answering many emergency calls and being constantly on the phone with the lab. I would come home, eat a big dinner, and pass out on the couch --too tired to play with Olivia. I started feeling unhealthy and then unhappy.

Clearly my clinical work model didn't scale well. Instead, the more cases we sold, the more I stayed in clinic. So I raised my prices. But that didn't matter. The cases kept coming in.

I started to cringe every time another patient accepted a big case. I started encouraging patients to shop around. That they could get the same work done at the practice across the street for a lower cost. That was *not* a good sign.

Burnt-out and out of shape, I decided it was time to listen to what my wife was saying all along.

It was time to start an online course.

The moment I decided to launch an online course, it revived me. I felt the adrenaline flow through my veins again. I told the receptionist to block any days on the schedule that were not yet booked. No more new patients. And I also told her that her new job was learning Mailchimp and how to use it to build an audience.

Alvin and I hoisted a dental chair from one of the ops and into the sterilization area for storage. Then, I turned that op into a recording studio with a huge whiteboard of all the videos I had to make in order to complete an online course teaching the fundamentals of implant surgery.

I spent every working hour I could inside that room. I turned into that crazy robed homeless person again, only emerging from my bunker to refill my coffee or to see the patients that still somehow found their way onto the schedule.

I also found myself playing musical chairs with my dad. Having a dental office with only one operatory didn't make any sense to him. I tried to explain that I needed a recording studio. He would shoot back a bewildered look—probably thinking that the stress had finally gotten to his son. So he insisted.

So every time he visited, we would move the chair back to the operatory, but sure enough, me and Alvin would move it back out so I could record more videos for my course.

I poured my heart into building that course. Within it, I saw my opportunity to create that beautiful, meaningful product.

This was my opportunity to redeem myself for all of the failed projects and hustles. To create something that I could be proud of. This was how I was going to build my implant business.

It was time to go big or go home. And what was bigger than the state dental convention?

We would reveal our course to the world at the California Dental Association meeting in San Francisco. We spent $10,000 to arrange to be at the dental meeting as an exhibitor. I informed our little team that I was not taking any patient's at all for the next month.

More coffee. More crazy man in the bunker.

In our hotel, our team rehearsed our sales pitch over and over.

That morning I put on a navy blue suit and was ready to sell. Then, it was our time to shine.

But something was off. People came to our booth to take pictures and meet the Implant Ninja team. They bought books, but nobody cared about our courses!

They said:

"An online course? For implants? How can you possibly teach surgery online? Not interested."

We managed to sell a grand total of 3 enrollments at the conference.

I felt rejected...stupid, embarrassed.

I kept a smile on during the event but sulked in the evening.

I thought about all the time I spent on this. On the money we spent, on the money we missed by stopping our clinic. On the opportunity cost of working on this. I was a dad now, and my family needed me. I poured our resources into this thing that looked like it was...nothing but a dream.

I thought back to ALL of my failed ideas. To all of the time I had wasted, working on projects that never amounted to much.

Instability.

I confided in Alvin, "What the hell are we gonna do man? I put everything into this."

Alvin, a man of few words, sat quietly before replying, "We'll get there. We just have to keep at it."

Throughout the "launch" weekend, we did get some sales from Instagram. Thank God for those 27 hardcore IG fans who purchased. Bless them. I would have gone crazy if they hadn't validated that SOMEBODY cared.

In my disappointment, I became so self-absorbed that I left my team to clean up, break down and pack up our stuff on their own.

As a matter of fact, I can hardly call them a team, because I was a terrible leader. I wasn't mean or rude but, I didn't know how to inspire, I didn't put their needs first.

Like a child, it was all about what 'I' wanted—what Ivan needed.

I'm ashamed of the leader that I was, but hey, we didn't learn about leadership or how to build a company while in dental school.

So on Monday morning, I wandered into work in a trance. If my team was looking for direction, all they got from me was mumbled, half-replies.

I lumbered over to the operatory/bunker. I locked the door behind me, grabbed an expo pen, and sat and stared into my whiteboard.

CHAPTER 9

I became a different person after that CDA convention. My boyish optimism gone.

In its place, a bitter realism.

Up until that point, I had held out hope that one of my projects would be a big success.

That if I tried enough, this manic pursuit would lead me somewhere meaningful. But I started to think that maybe all the realists were right. Maybe these big ambitions and successes were not for someone like me. Maybe I simply wasn't smart enough.

I should have just been working 6 days a week in clinic like my dad had said.

I struck me how lonely entrepreneurship could be. You put in countless hours and emotional investment hoping that in the end you will be vindicated by success. You work in hopes that you will eventually see the fruit of your labor. That you will

someday find proof that you were right and that all that time spent building and sacrificing...was worth it.
But if that proof never comes...

...well then maybe you were just a fool, I thought to myself.

I imagined the bigwigs at dental school laughing at the piles of money that I now owed them. I sure felt like a damned fool.

I stopped shaving. I wore wrinkled shirts and sandals to work. My hair a disheveled mess.

One day, as I walked to my car to go to the office, my neighbor Joe yelled, "HEY!! YOUR SPRINKLERS ARE ON TOO LONG! IT'S MESSING WITH MY GRASS!!"

He always seemed to be yelling at me about something in those days.

I felt like all I needed was a kid on a bike to stop in front of my house and kick me in the shins. And for a cat to throw up on my lawn—as Joe's cats frequently did.

I was lost.

With no direction from me, my team wondered what they should be doing. Not knowing what else to do, I cut their hours in the dental clinic—and I didn't even have the nerve to tell them myself. I asked Teresa to do it. One by one, the employees of our little clinic left.

The woman who served as the receptionist, shouted at Teresa in rage. Insulted that we had cut her hours, her voice shook every room of our entire little office space before she stormed off.

Then, only Alvin remained.

Trusty Alvin, for some reason he still believed we could become something great. I never understood why he had so much faith. He would have charged in to battle with me, without asking why.

He was very much my opposite. Stable. Reliable. Supremely organized. A CrossFit junkie, his massive presence brought a sense of gravity with it. It felt as if Alvin were along for the ride, it must be a worthy endeavor. I was lucky to have joined forces with him early on.

Unfortunately, me and him were not enough to keep our practice running. One patient that came in for an implant consultation told his referring doctor that he didn't want to come back to us because our office felt empty.

It was.

I brainstormed what the hell to do.

I needed to keep making the student loan payments, but how could I go about it now that I realized the limitations of my practice and of my online business.

As I tended to do under periods of uncertainty, I ran in ten different directions to see what opportunities presented themselves.

I applied to join the army, looked for dental practices to buy, looked at associate positions out of the state, I pitched the faculty at my alma mater on using my online learning platform (they said no), I applied for implant instructor positions at other dental universities, I looked into how I could take doctors to Guatemala to train them in implant surgery, I researched further into starting an implant company but I got stuck at the FDA compliance again, and was always I looking for more jobs.

I worked through all of these options on my whiteboard. And just like in dental school, my plan slowly revealed itself .

1. First, we needed to stop trying to run our own clinic. That was not what I enjoyed or was good at. Instead, all effort would go towards creating clinical content and building up Implant Ninja Education. Having my own clinic was not the goal. Building Implant Ninja Education was.
2. I needed to write the second edition of the All on X Handbook. People loved the first edition and would surely appreciate an update.
3. We needed to create more online courses and they needed to be the best in the industry. Anybody could build an online course, but ours needed to be the best.

Now that I had some sort of plan, I did a post-mortem on my launch at CDA. Although I was still seething from failure, I tried to filter some lessons from it.

The first lesson was to "Give them the fish." When you go into a restaurant and order fish, you expect to get a delicious fish meal without having to cook it yourself. You probably don't want the chef to invite you to the kitchen to cook it for yourself. You just want to eat.

Likewise, in business, it is easier to sell someone something they already want, instead of trying to convince them they need something different. I had read this in The $100 start up but I didn't *really* get it till then.

Go where the fish are. If you want to make any sales, you need to go where people already want what you offer. An in-person trade expo is not where people are looking to buy an online course. These people wanted physical goods, not online courses. I needed to alter where I making my sales pitch.

So, with a clearer vision, and some new lessons, we decided to hit the gas full speed. We were going to go hardcore in clinic and hardcore on Implant Ninja. Burning the candle on both ends. I worked like a man possessed and brought in a ton of clinical cases.

As if to hit the refresh button, I searched for another implant company to work with. I decided to go with Neodent because everyone else on social media was trying them out. The rep was a really nice guy, although he was a bit persistent about getting me to close the sale. Before I did, I asked if he could help me to become a speaker for their brand. I had asked the same of Zimmer previously, but nothing came of it, because everyone quit on me. He promised he would.

So, I bought a $15,000 Neodent starter kit. It was a decent kit. I enjoyed using it for full mouth reconstructive cases. And the rep got me a local speaking gig. However, local gigs were not what I was after. I wanted to get broad exposure for Implant Ninja. I wanted word to spread about our brand and the educational platform we were building.

But, as I didn't have enough pictures of Neodent cases, there was a limit to how effectively I could speak on their implants.

So I got to work placing their implants and cataloging my cases, hoping that it would lead to bigger speaking opportunities.

However, the goal was to gradually phase out of running our own clinic and transition to full time Implant Ninja Education. To do that we needed to continue our marathon in clinic and we needed to simultaneously build and improve our online course offering.

Me and Alvin couldn't do all the heavy lifting ourselves.

So, we brought on another ninja.

As I sifted through hundreds of resumes, one name: Excelie, stood out from all the applicants. I invited her for an interview the next day. Immediately I could tell how organized and composed she was. With how much of a disorganized mess I was, Implant Ninja needed all the composure we could gather. We needed a massive influx of composure immediately.

So, I hired her right away. The interview was the day before Christmas. I asked her if she could start work the next day. She said, 'No problem.'

We were able to get our clinical production level back to normal, doing around $35,000 per month. I spent this time slowly building our new course: The All on X Online Course and I worked on finishing the second edition of the All on X book.

Next, I hired a freelance videographer that would follow me around and make content out of my clinical days. I challenged him to "Make my day seem interesting!"

For the first time in my short career, I started to feel some momentum. Cases were coming in, Alvin and Excelie were building the Implant Ninja brand. And up until then, Olivia had always kept us on our toes, but Teresa had now hit a good stride with her at home. It wasn't easy, but under Teresa's care, Olivia was thriving.

It felt like the right time for me to jump in and make as much money as I could to pay down my debt.

So, just like in Michigan, I started working again as a travelling implant placer. I would drive around 2 days per week placing about 6-10 implants per day. My route included local DSO offices as well as private general dental clinics. Once again, I was the barber-surgeon, rolling in with my Home Depot toolbox full of scalpels, drills, and implants.

One of the offices I frequented was in the heart of San Francisco's Chinatown. It was a totally different ballgame. The pace was so fast, I had to bring Alvin along for the ride. We would run two, often three rooms. He would do implant restorations in one chair, and I would do surgeries in another.

The office provided a second assistant, Jenny, who would barter the cost of the implant with the patients. Jenny and the patients would yell at each other like they were haggling for a ginseng at the farmers market. After a fierce shouting match in Cantonese, Jenny would turn to me and say, "Okay, he's ready to place implant."

On the 2-hour drive home, Alvin and I were zombies. We'd often stop at the half-way point, to get a greasy burger and recount the day's adventures. Our conversations were full of blood, acrylic, and crazy patient tales.

By June 2019, I was on fire. Our patient base was providing enough clinical production to bring about that coveted state: stability. On top of that, driving around and placing implants for other offices was allowing me to pay off big chunks of my student loans. Forget paying $8,300 a month. I was throwing $15,000 each month at that debt.

And the icing on the cake is that the second edition of the All on X Handbook completely sold out when we offered it online.

I was Marty from the show, The Ozarks. I owed money to the cartel and was finding any means necessary to pay it back. And now it was finally flowing.

Our team was totally crushing it. We focused on creating quality implant educational content and making it as widely available as possible. We were on track to building something great. I was even able to start ordering product samples for the future implant company that I wanted to build.

Our team was clear on our mission:

To create the best online implant learning resources in the world.

Stability. Growth.

I was not earning the $400,000 that I initially thought, but I was happy.

Teresa was happy. Olivia was stable. She still had a large mass on her face and neck, but we were peaceful.

In an email to my parents, I wrote:

"My long-term goal is to be in a place where I can continue to do good work. I don't want to keep raising production goals. I just want to be stable and happy with the work that I am doing. For me, more clinical production will not justify taking additional days away from my family and other endeavors."

Olivia had been stable for a while now. She was a happy and rambunctious two-year-old.

But now, she was starting to notice that people looked at her differently. She noticed when kids would point and laugh or call her a monster and run away on the playground.

She would just stare at them, stunned.

These moments left Teresa heartbroken. Olivia was a confident and happy little girl, and Teresa didn't want that to change.

So, with this new sense of momentary peace in our lives, Teresa suggested we push forward with the next stage of treatment for Oli so that by the time she started school, her self-esteem would stay intact.

Olivia's condition is one that does not have a definitive treatment. People with lymphatic malformations live with them for their entire lives. And all the tissue in the affected area continues to grow disproportionately. However, there were many different treatments that might improve her condition. Several with serious risks. Fearing these risks, we had played it safe until now.

But now, with some mental clarity to think through the options, we thought it was time to move forward to give her a chance at a better life.

So, I sat in my garage with a white board in front of me. I listed out the best doctors in the country who specialized in lymphatic malformations. One of the names on the board came from my mom. She said that she had been praying about it and had found a doctor named Jonathan Perkins out of Seattle, Washington. Consult after consult, the doctors each told us what they would do for Olivia. And their plans all differed from one another's. Some wanted to inject alcohol into her cheek. Others recommended scarring the tissue down with antibiotics or putting her on immunosuppressant medication.

Dr. Perkins suggested a big surgery called a neck resection. He had a lot of experience with these types of cases and thought that this was the best option for her. They would remove a big chunk from her neck and face. We were afraid, but we put our trust in Seattle Children Hospital and Dr. Perkins and we set the date for October 2019.

We had 3 months to get my things in order for this huge life event. I slowly wound down my clinic, I finished my cases at my door-to-door implant gigs and focused on finishing The All on X Online Course in time for the October "launch", which is what we called our new course or book releases.

I was pausing most of my income, so I needed to make sure I was still able to provide stability. I wanted October 2019 to be a successful launch so that Teresa wouldn't have to worry about anything but Olivia's care. So, I doubled down hard on Implant Ninja.

In October, right before we opened up our courses for enrollment, I posted this quote on the Implant Ninja Instagram story:

Shallow men believe in luck and circumstance…Strong men believe in cause and effect.

I felt like a strong man. And I was going to will this to happen.

I clicked "publish" on our website and then I opened up my Gmail inbox waiting for purchase confirmations.

I was instantly vindicated.

Email after email of purchases. In that week, we earned $130,000 in revenue for our 2 online courses and people who purchased the courses were immediately giving our courses rave reviews!

But the best gift during this time, came in an unexpected form. Teresa found out she was pregnant. It caught us totally by surprise. It had taken us years of trying before we were blessed with Olivia.

And now, God, karma, the world, was blessing us once more. Olivia would become a big sister.

We needed this—the emotional and financial reservoir of strength for what came immediately next, as Teresa and I walked with Olivia into Seattle Children's Hospital for her big surgery.

CHAPTER 10

Teresa and I felt strong.

We were determined to push through this upcoming phase of treatment for Olivia. We felt that it would be manageable. We expected that it might be a bit difficult. That we would have to pamper Olivia for a few months, and that we would lose some sleep, but that with some extra TLC—it would all be okay.

And we were certain that this was the time to do it. Before all the finger-pointing and staring slowly eroded our little girl's self-esteem.

It was done in two steps. The first step was to remove her tonsils and adenoids. We booked an Airbnb in Bellevue, Washington. A quiet little house near a nature trail. The crisp autumn air in the pacific northwest was a refreshing change. It felt like a cabin in the woods.

We stayed up late with Olivia, eating snacks and watching TV because we needed her to wake up early and not eat the next morning before her surgery.

In the early morning we strolled her, sleepy-eyed, to the operating wing of the hospital. By the time Teresa and I finished up our coffees, Olivia was done. It was quick. She was in and out in an hour. She recovered immediately after her procedure. As soon as the anesthesia wore off, she was back to normal.

We were told to expect the same recovery process for the second surgery—the neck resection. Back in Michigan, I had assisted for neck resections. The skin of the patient's neck is literally flapped backwards, exposing all the internal anatomy. Then, bits and chunks and bits of tissue are dissected and cut away.

It sure didn't seem like someone could recover from that quickly. The thought this being done to Olivia made me nauseous.

For this second phase of surgery, we again booked an Airbnb, and had the most wonderful night before the procedure.

There was a window above our bed. The three of us searched for shooting stars before drifting off to sleep.

Just like before, we strolled her into the surgical wing, feeling optimistic. We told her that she would get lollipops after her procedure. She was so excited. She knew that the first surgery had gone fine, and so she wasn't scared at all of this second surgery.

And we waved goodbye as they rolled her away on a hospital bed. In her yellow hospital gown, she smiled and waved back.

The procedure was supposed to take about 6-7 hours. Teresa and I walked around, had lunch, waited, and prayed.

We tried not to obsess over the screen on the wall that has the patient status updates. Hoping we wouldn't see any alerts pop up on the screen.

6 hours pass, then 7, then 9..

Then 10 hours pass.

We were beside ourselves. A dread gnawing within. The hospital clerk's reply didn't do much to calm our worries, "They're still in surgery. I don't have any more information."

Finally, Olivia's bed was rolled out.

I had been recording the journey on a handheld camera. So I turned my camera on to film her but as soon as I caught a glimpse of her, my hands collapsed and the camera fell.

As she was rolled out on the hospital bed, she sat there looking stunned. I knew that anesthesia has this effect, but this was something else. It was different.

She looked mortified. Like she had just seen a ghost. Like she had no clue what the hell was going on.

Her head was wrapped in a blue bandage, her tongue was inflated and sticking out of her mouth, her face was a balloon caricature, and blood was seeping into all the bandages around her neck. A sliver of skin missing from her right temple, from where a staple had been placed. Her hair was tangled with sticky knots of blood.

She sat there on the bed, not moving. Motionless. Eyes fixated forward.

Before the surgery, we had told her she could have a lollipop once it was done. It looked to me like she wouldn't be able to eat anything for weeks.

The had apparently removed more tissue than they had anticipated—which was a good thing. But they were unable to remove some lymphatic malformation tissue at the base of her skull because it was too dangerous. So, some was left behind.

Dr. Perkins, the man who had just run this surgical marathon with our daughter, sat across from us. Beads of sweat building up under his surgical cap as he spoke. I could tell he had given all that he possibly could.

It had ended up being a difficult procedure for him and for her. But if that was it, then we could have gotten through it. I understood what normal surgical recoveries were like.

I had some experience with smaller surgeries in my office and understood that surgical recoveries are a difficult time but they have a normal progression and that people recover. They might feel beat up, but it's just a matter of time before patients feel good as new.

But for Olivia, it was different.

We stayed in the hospital intensive care area. A little room that was thoughtfully decorated with fish, and whales, and other things that kids like.

Olivia still sat there, stunned.

The playful decorations, the Disney movies and songs, the dinosaur stickers—felt eerie when juxtaposed with Olivia's blood-soaked bandages.

She had just lost a lot of blood and was still losing it, so she got a blood transfusion.

Slowly Olivia learned to become terrified. She learned that every 2 to 3 hours, somebody would come in and poke her and change her bandages—which was especially painful because of the dried blood sticking to everything. This would continue around the clock. And so Olivia learned to be afraid in the night that somebody was coming to get her.

She became distrustful of everyone except me and Teresa. She would only sleep if we were holding her. So, we split up shifts and alternated resting periods.

One night, when I was on the early shift (9PM-3AM), I was trying to distract myself with Netflix when Olivia threw up in her sleep. She was not able to properly cough, or even move her tongue because of the surgical trauma. She waved her hands around in panic. She looked to me to help her, because she couldn't help herself.

Not knowing what to do, I grabbed her leg, and swung it up above my head—flipping her upside down. She dangled in the air with her IV tubing and all the sensors hanging off of her.

Then I slammed the palm of my hand on her back to try to dislodge whatever fluids or things she had stuck in her throat.

She was panicking and pointing at her throat. I flipped her right side up again, and ran out of the room and sprinted down the hospital corridor in search of a nurse. I told them I needed a suction immediately. They told me not to worry and that it was not likely that Olivia would aspirate and that she looked fine.

But it didn't seem right to me. She was panicking and making strange noises from her throat, I got the suction and Olivia shoved it in her throat and got chunks the vomit that were lingering. I don't know what was the right thing to do in that situation. But when you see your child suffering, you do what you need to do to try to fix it as fast as you can.

She was a trooper. She tried to keep her spirit up. But she was down. The entire time. Teresa and I would try to distract her. But after a while, kids get sick of the iPad. When you're living at the hospital for months, kids don't want an iPad, stickers, or toys anymore. Instead, they begin to stare out the window. They want their freedom.

Her spirit was slowly crumbling.

When her spirit began to pick up, she would point out of the door. She wanted to explore the hospital. So would take her out with a little red wagon, and walk around the hospital floor and collect little pieces of hospital tape from each nurses stations to make a bracelet. We would put her in a wheelchair and push her really fast down an empty hall at night pretending it was a race car.

Both Teresa's parents and my parents came out to visit us while she was recovering. Olivia adored them. They were able to have some good times despite the hardship. Olivia's eyes would light-up when my dad would play the "Eye of the

Tiger" and all grandparents would cheer her on as she thrust her tiny fist in the air to the music.

She was on heavy duty pain medication, but we still spent the entire time distracting her from her pain. Unable to eat even the softest foods, she seemed to get joy from feeding us the Jello she was served.

After a while, we were moved from the intensive care area, to the regular surgical recovery section of the hospital. It felt like we sort of moved further and further down the hospital, and didn't get that much attention after a while. And so one day we asked if we could go home. The nurse seemed unsure but he let us go that day.

We packed up and moved to a hotel, happy to be back in the real world again. But that night Olivia's face started to swell up like a balloon. Like an actual balloon. It swelled to the point that I was afraid that the swelling was compressing her blood vessels. I was afraid that this pressure was causing damage. It looked like that balloon that was about to pop.

We called the emergency team. But it was unclear whether we should go in or not. It always happens on the weekends. On the weekends, hospitals tend to have different teams than the ones during the week. You just speak to the doctor on call and they're usually not familiar with your case so they always say, "I can't say for sure, but if you are afraid that this is serious, all I can say is you should come in."

This seems simple enough, but the emergency room process itself is traumatic for children. The last thing I wanted to do, while Olivia's face was a balloon, and she was distraught from the pain, was to take her to go get poked and prodded and have her endure sitting in an ER room for 3 hours in the middle of the night.

She was already sad enough. She was already traumatized. She literally was too afraid to sleep without being held, every single night.

We decided to wait for her regular team, who would be there in the morning. We still had to go through the ER process, but this way her surgeon was able to evaluate her. He made the decision to take her to the OR to drain her face right away.

They made another incision and this time they stuck a tube inside. It was called a JP drain, and it was a plastic tube with a little bulb at the end. Every day that little bulb would fill up with blood and we had to prevent the hose from becoming clogged with blood. So, every day we had to milk the tube, we would squeeze it so that the blood comes out of Olivia's neck, like juice from a straw and empty into the reservoir bulb.

The bulb was the size of an apple. And every day that thing was full of blood. She was losing all that blood every day. The doctor said that most patients keep it no longer than 1 month. Olivia had it in for months. She just keep draining non-stop.

She was a generally a good sport. She allowed people to draw her blood. She'd let them poke her 2 maybe 3 times. But if they keep poking her, and they're not successful at getting a vain, Teresa and I would get fed up and tell the nurse, "Go get the phlebotomist, phlebotomists only." But every time, the nurse would reply, "You know, I'm pretty good at this. I'm gonna get it don't worry."

And every time, after 5 pokes, they call in the phlebotomist.

One day, in her sleep, Olivia accidentally pulled out the feeding tube from her nose. And when she wouldn't let the nurse put it back in, 3 nurses pinned her down to the bed and rolled her up in a mat. This effectively immobilized her arms, but it had an effect on her that I'll never forget.

She thrashed and thrashed as her eyes turned black from her pupils dilating so wide. And then suddenly, she stopped. She gave up. She had no more fight and no more tears. She laid there, lifeless and pale with black eyes, staring at nothing, as the nurse inserted the yellow tube that went into her nose and down her throat.

These things were really hard to go through.

What I remember the most was carrying her nonstop. She was too afraid to be by herself. In too much pain to sleep. Too uncomfortable and paranoid that someone would come poke her more.

So, Teresa and I would take turns carrying her most of the day—but especially the whole night.

At nighttime, she would get woken up every 2 hours so I would carry her on my shoulder the entire time, because otherwise she was too afraid to sleep.

I would stay up the entire night carrying her, watching movies to try to distract myself from the cold numbness coming from my shoulders. Leaning on things to try to lessen the pain.

It was a test of will. For both me and Teresa.

Both of us were completely depleted, but we had to pull ourselves through this process. You would think that we would offer each other some hope, some resilience. But I was dead and just giving everything I had leftover. And she did the same. She gave everything she possibly could. No happiness leftover. Just all anguish. And fear.

Looking at Olivia's misery. We wondered, *What the hell did we do?*

Did we make a mistake?
Did we just cripple our daughter?

Who knew?

I think the process took 6 months. But I really don't know. It could have taken an entire year. Maybe that's not true, but I don't know. The reason is that it didn't have a clear ending. It spilled over into the rest of our lives for years.

Her postoperative surgery recovery was one thing. Normally at the end of the surgical recovery, you're done, you're good, or at least you're better.

But that a wasn't the case for us. That's why it turns from 6 months, to a year, to a year and half, to 2 years. All that time, it was never truly "better."

It felt like a never-ending battle. It felt like we were stuck in a nightmare. And nobody could help. The world went on without us.

I never once doubted Dr. Perkin's surgical skills or compassion as a doctor. I knew he was doing the best that was possible—this was just the hand that we had been dealt.

During this entire time, I still had to work. Still had to pay that debt. I still owed the cartel.

While Teresa could technically could have worked; she was 1000% focused on Olivia's recovery. That's where she felt she needed to be.

Teresa was so tough during this entire process. I don't remember her once complaining. I know her tank was completely depleted.

We tried to be strong for one another. We were thoroughly depleted but we never vocalized it. But at the end of each night, we secretly cried – each one of us not wanting the other to find out.

We were in Washington, a state where I was not licensed as a dentist, but I had to find a way to make an income. I would find moments to escape on my computer for an hour here or there so that I could still connect with my team in California and find a way to help keep Implant Ninja running. Teresa could handle all of Olivia's care on her own, but I found it hard to break myself away. I felt an emotional duty to stay in the suffering. It felt wrong to abandon them.

But, by breaking away for short work trips, I was able to bring in some much needed income. I was the caveman going out for T-Rex meat.

I had made these arrangements with some big dental corporations and implant companies where I would fly out and train their doctors to do dental implant procedures. I would do seminars and workshops. And it was fantastic because that was one of my favorite things to do, and it helped keep us afloat financially.

Trusty Alvin would usually accompany me to these workshops. We would always put on a great seminar. And we'd celebrate with a couple of Moscow Mules at the hotel bar. For a moment, I'd allow myself to forget the struggle and have some good laughs. We'd talk about the implant company we someday build. Those lighthearted moments would keep me going. Keep me pushing, till the next one.

But every time flew out, I felt so guilty to leave Teresa to fend for herself. I felt guilty that I was able to sleep in a hotel room in a bed all to myself. Nevertheless, I found myself unable to sleep. I just thought about Teresa and Oli. And worried for them constantly.

One memory stands out in particular.

A year earlier, a national dental group had asked me to do a seminar all the way in Florida. This was one of the biggest dental groups in the country, so it was a great opportunity for our brand. And it was almost time for me to fly out for it.

By this time, we were staying a place called the Ronald McDonald House, or RMC, which was a place that families could stay while their children were undergoing hospital treatment. Olivia had befriended a couple of the older kids during a game of hide and seek at the cafeteria.

These children were truly suffering. There was no doubt about it. You could tell just by looking at them. Their pale faces. Their scars and bare heads. Their wheelchairs. Their backpacks which drip fed them or provided an infusion of medications.

When a little boy named Ryan stopped mid-play to say hi to Olivia, she looked down. She was shy about the tube in her neck. He pulled down his shirt collar and showed her the tube sticking out of his chest. Olivia gave a little half smile, and joined in on the game of hide and seek.

When the children played, you could tell they were back to being just kids. They laughed like it was any other day. They were happy in spite of the tremendous suffering they experienced.

Despite the extreme hardship that the families endured, there was also warmth. There was *real* life.

So while Teresa was apprehensive about me flying so far away, she felt comfortable in the RMC community and she definitely didn't want me to cancel on prior commitments.

Before I left, our little family went to Nordstrom rack to buy a suit for me to wear. Although anyone would forgive me for not looking sharp, Teresa insisted that I wear a suit and give the best damn presentation I could.

I flew all the way across the country from Washington to Florida—the two extremes. Before flying there, the dental group had told me something to the effect of, "the implant company will take care of it, they're paying you, don't worry."

I gave a 3-hour seminar to an audience of 600. I concluded by telling the audience that Olivia was still recovering, and that it was actually her birthday. I recorded a video of the entire crowd singing happy birthday for her. All things considered; I thought I had given a great show.

I was feeling damn proud of myself.

After walking around to see some of the dental company booths at this meeting, I came across the booth for the implant company that had agreed to sponsor me for this event.

I thanked them for inviting me. I told them I looked forward to doing more events like this.

But they looked confused.

One of the women spoke up, "I'm sorry but I don't think we're paying you..."

Can you imagine flying across the country, knowing that my wife and daughter need me, and to think that I am not going to get paid?

They said they would sort it out with the dental group and get back to me. On the flight back to Washington the next morning, I got a text from Teresa. Back in Washington, Olivia hadn't been able to sleep. Her itchiness, her pain, and her night terrors had kept her screaming all night. My sister, Andrea, had booked a last minute flight to go help Teresa. When she arrived at 2AM, Teresa was able to step out of the house and go pick up medication for Olivia.

I didn't tell her about the questionable status of my payment.

I finally got an email confirmation that I would indeed be paid for the talk, but that left quite the impression on me.

"These companies really don't care about me", I thought to myself.

I was also still flying back to California once per month to place implants. At a minimum, no matter what had been going on in my life, I have always tried to keep that once per month implant marathon at my parent's office. And at this moment, I depended on it to survive.

On those trips, I was completely drained. In my already zombie sleep-deprived state, I'd arrive at home in Cali at midnight, and had to be up early the next morning, to put on a cheerful demeanor and be ready to see patients.

One day as I walked to my car in the morning, I noticed that all my plants in my yard had died, including the tree in front of my house. Having had enough complaining from my neighbor Joe, I had previously unplugged my damn sprinklers before leaving to Washington. The dead tree made it look like a haunted house.

As I unlocked the car, I heard his familiar holler, "HEY! WE GOT TO DO SOMETHING ABOUT YOUR LAWN!"

Joe was quite a character. Before he retired and elected himself as the unofficial neighborhood watch, he had worked at the state prison for many years—and it showed. He was loud and rough. He was the bain of door-door salesmen in our neighborhood. He would always yell at them, "I don't give a fuck who you are! Get off my property before I call security!" And he would sometimes chase them down the street with his shirt off.

He stalked over and explained that he wanted to redo our front yards so that my grass was more even with his grass to make it easier for him to park his boat. He handed me a bill for the yard work that he wanted me to help pay for.

"That's not my problem Joe." I muttered—only half paying attention to him. He was always so opinionated about my lawn. I invited him into my garage to set the dials on the sprinkler system to his liking. Then I went off to work.

Having to do consultations during this time felt like torture. I would listen to people complain about their tooth shade or complain about their previous dentist. They would stick their fingers in their mouth to show me their problems. But I simply did not care. I tried to be courteous, but my eyes gave me away. To help me get through these listening sessions, I would dig my the fingernail of my thumb into my index finger. The angrier I was, the harder I pushed.

I thought about the children back at the hospital. The children with massive scars on their head. With tubes sticking out of their chest…and neck.

Those felt like real problems.

Behind my mask, through clenched teeth, I listened.

I remember one morning as I got ready for clinic, I looked at my face in the mirror and I didn't recognize who I saw looking back. My face was blotchy red, my eyes devoid of any emotion. I didn't see myself. I saw a deranged stranger.

In clinic, I would resort to splashing cold water on my face and slapping myself hard to become more alert so I could keep pushing through the day. I took my coffee like I was taking a shot of tequila. That day in clinic, after my ritualistic slapping of the face and psyching myself up to "wake up" more–I developed an extra heartbeat. And it scared the shit out of me. After work I went to the ER. The doctor told me that extra heartbeats are normal in times of stress.

He advised me to reduce my stress.

Luckily my team at Implant Ninja was holding it down. Far from falling apart, things were humming along.

We had a successful enrollment period for our online courses prior to the surgery and through this, I was still finding time to do zoom meetings with my team. It was a way for me to stay sane. To distract myself a bit. And indulge a little bit in my passion for implants. Even though it seemed totally unimportant compared to what we were going through at that point in our lives.

I once read a quote by Woodrow Wilson that read something like, "I use all the brains I have and all that I can borrow." In those days I learned to rely heavily on borrowing other people's brains—especially Alvin's. Sleep deprived I would often tell him over the phone, "Listen man, you are thinking more clearly than me these days. You make the decision. Do what is best for the brand."

Keeping Implant Ninja was fun for me and it helped me to feel useful. To feel like, I am doing this and I am paying my daughters medical bills. That I was not holding back anything that my daughter needs.

That drove me.

It helped me get through this part. As I think on that now, I realize that Teresa didn't have that.

She was all in with Olivia's care. She didn't have an outlet. All she knew was to take care of Olivia. I was trying to take care of both of them, but I was trying not to break myself. I felt like I had nothing left to give. But Teresa kept going. So I kept going.

CHAPTER 11

It's funny how life happens in phases. Sometimes things are wonderful – but you often don't realize just how wonderful it is in that moment. Then something happens, and it can turn your life upside down. Then you think back to "the good old days" and long to return to that sense of normalcy.

A happy life, or success in life, doesn't occur in a linear progression. Instead, it looks more like a rollercoaster, and hopefully you can make good decisions that lead you on an upwards trend towards...*stability*.

This next phase in my life was characterized by some semi-stability. Olivia was still freshly recovered from her surgery but we had now been finally able to return to our home in California. We were still afraid to let our guard down. Fearing that we would plunge back into instability. After all, we had already once made our grand return to California, only to rush back to Washington within 1 week to urgently drain Olivia's face.

The sleep deprivation and cortisol in my veins made me a loose cannon—more than I normally already was. One day as I carried Olivia to the car, I heard Joe's holler once more.

"HEY BAMBINO!," A term he had taken to calling me as I was the younger guy on the block, "YOUR TRASH BINS HAVE BEEN OUT FOR 2 DAYS! AND YOUR SPRINKLERS ARE STILL MESSING UP MY LAWN. YOU NEED TO FIX YOUR YARD SO IT DOESN'T DEVALUE THE NEIGHBORHOOD!"

I glared at him, like a rabid animal.

I set Olivia down.

I walked straight up to him. Squaring my shoulders to his. He took two steps back so that he was back on his lawn.

I took a step forward. My knuckles white and ready to come crashing down on this man's face.

"What the fuck are you talking about?," I dared him to make me mad.

He held up his hands and said, "WHOA! I'm not looking to fight…"

I saw myself standing there, on another man's property, ready to punch him. And realized I was out of control.

I relaxed my first and let the air out of my lungs.

I told him about all the shit we had just gone through. And that I didn't have time to deal with this. I told him not to give me bullshit because I don't tolerate it. But, I told him that he was right about the lawn. And we had a good hard laugh about what a piece of shit my lawn was.

We were now in this reluctant steady state. Clearly, I could still snap at any moment. It wasn't peace, but it was some respite from the terror we had just endured.

And speaking of terror, Olivia still couldn't sleep. She still had night terrors. It was more than that. It was full blown PTSD. And so, we still didn't sleep.

To avoid being woken in the middle of the night by her screams, I stayed awake into the small hours of the night, reading deeper and deeper about implants.

It turns out the history of implants took a rollercoaster journey over the decades as well.

The story starts back in the early civilizations. The ingenuity of people that we would consider primitive, is nothing short of astonishing.

I can start the story, ironically, at the place of my birth – Peru. It was the home of the Incas, who were an ancient civilization of great warriors, architects, engineers,…and surgeons.

They built their cities way up in the mountains, with boulders the size of cars. But, there were no boulders nearby for them to build with. So, they had to *drag* them uphill for miles. More astonishingly, they were able to neatly cut corners into these rocks and stack them with Tetris-like precision. These are unbelievable feats. My grandfather would often ask me to run my hands over the joints of these boulders to see if I could find imperfections. I couldn't. He asked me how it was possible. With his squint in his eyes, and a half-smile, he would me if I thought they might have been built by an extraterrestrial life-form.

I think he somehow secretly knew how they did it. I think he had some Inca blood running through his veins.

The Incas also performed skull surgeries. I'm not sure if this was for some ritual or to cure a disease, but they would often cut large holes or windows through their patient's skulls. And in the modern day we have found evidence that patients often survived these surgeries because the recovered skeletons show skulls with healed bone in the surgical sites.

In other parts of Latin America, civilizations such as the Mayans and tribes in Honduras would carve rocks and seashells and implant them into the jawbone. And the seashells would actually integrate into the jaw!

In my book, *they* were the first ones to discover osseointegration.

Throughout the 1800's and early 1900's dentists tinkered with different implant designs. They treated patients during the day and invented their own implants at night. They bent wire, casted metal, whittled cow teeth, melted rubber, all to try to figure out the magical mix of material and design that would allow them to stick a foreign body into human bone and build a tooth on top.

If you look back to the designs made by two Americans—the Strock brothers—back in the 1940's, they look almost exactly like the implants that we have on the market today! Although they made them from a material called Vitallium.

But, like I said, implants took many crazy turns. In Europe people started bending wire to make the 'spiral implant'. In Sweden, Dr. Dahl invented what he called the 'subperiosteal implant', which is basically a metal cage that sits on top of the jaw, but the dental society prohibited him from pursuing it! They claimed it was too controversial.

Dentists everywhere were trying to find the best design.

And then, there was the discovery of titanium osseointegration.

Implant lore credits this discovery to PI Brannemark. But actually, this accomplishment was achieved by Levanthal, who discovered it a year prior to when Brannemark coined the term "osseointegration."

Brannemark found one of those perfect, rare situations in which the stars align. The Swedish government funded his research on dental implants. He was able to experiment and design and perform surgeries, all funded by the government.

This proved to be pivotal for the history of implantology. It provided the research that established the titanium screw as the gold standard for dental implants.

And the rest is history.

The companies Nobel Pharma and Straumann were born in this time. And shortly after that, a young prosthodontist named, Gerald Niznick created an implant called Core-Vent, which became the flagship product for Zimmer, and then he founded Implant Direct which ended up dominating the American marketplace.

After that, there were no more tinkerers. No more inventors. The industry had become big businesses competing against even bigger businesses.

Virtually every implant company was gobbled up by a massive multi-national company—each with a massive sales army. These whales would almost always own a handful of implant companies so that they could perform the strategically profitable practice of price discrimination.

Gone were the days where a dentist would pull an implant out of their pocket and explain to you the benefits of their design. Now it was sales representatives who had just gone through crash course on how to sell implants, who were now explaining why their implant was the better than implant x,y,z.

These nights I would piece this story together from many different sources. Pulling bits of information from reading, and some from conversations I had with old school veterans of the industry.

As I learned more, the rich history started to come alive.

And with it, I came alive too.

I began to see, for the first time, how I, Ivan Chicchon, could fit into this history. And where Implant Ninja could make a real impact.

I had many sleepless nights to ponder this.

CHAPTER 12

Covid wrecked many things for countless people. It was hard time to be sure. It stole many loved ones, collapsed many businesses, and changed everyone's lives.

But for Implant Ninja, 2020 started off in relative peace.

No longer being able to work out of the 150 square foot consultation room at my parent's dental clinic (because it was shut down), we found a 450 square foot location by my house to rent out. It wasn't even a real unit, it was more of a tiny breakroom–but it would do.

For the last 2 years, Implant Ninja had doubled it's revenue each year. And this year, being unable to maintain my regular routine of hopping into a dental clinic for an implant surgery marathon a couple times a month, I once again decided to double down on Implant Ninja's growth.

We brought on board a talented young kid named Erick, who claimed to be a graphic designer.

He had been working at a preschool, when I invited him to interview with us. Clean cut and uber polite, we actually didn't even know he arrived for the initial interview because he just patiently sat in the waiting room of my parent's dental clinic.

"Already ten minutes late, this guy's not one of us." Alvin told Excelie before he realized that Erick had already been waiting there for half an hour.

Erick was able to recreate our entire brand and elevate our image.

Up until then, all the graphics were just my half-assed scribbles on my tablet. But Erick had an eye for great design and was able to use it to make everything we did look better. It was just what our brand needed.

Once I realized this, I started to tell him, "Make it up to 'Erick quality', not 'Ivan quality'" as my designs always looked like I made them in 5 minutes—which I did.

We also brought on a girl who was coincidentally one of Olivia's school teachers.

When I saw her application pop up on my phone inbox, I got confused.

"One of Olivia's teachers is applying for Implant Ninja? Does she know that she applied for a job with us?" I asked Teresa.

"That's funny. I wonder why we get so many applications from people who work at schools?" I asked and then put my phone away.
But Teresa wanted more details so I read the resume aloud as Teresa drove.

"You *need* to hire her. She seems perfect." Teresa said.

And so we hired Nikki Cruz.

Teresa has a sixth sense about these things. Although she is good at always seeing the best in people, she also has a great gut feeling about whether I could trust someone or not.

With a bubbly, sometimes over-the-top silly, personality, Nikki became the bedrock for our customer service. Over the years she evolved into a highly capable, still bubbly, leader within Implant Ninja.

But, it wasn't always smooth sailing with Implant Ninja.

Actually, like my personal life, it seems the business always alternated between stability and instability. Between exciting growth and fear of impending doom.

During this time, I approached a certain big implant company—one of the top 3 companies. We had talked before, and I had purchased from them in the past. They were supposed to help me get some speaking engagements. But that ended up not leading anywhere. So, I thought perhaps a partnership between the implant company and our online education platform could hold some promise.

Over the course of many months, I met with their VPs and supervisors of this and that. One time they came to my parent's office for lunch. Another time we went out to get coffee. These were all very high-level individuals flying from different parts of the country to take time to meet with me. One was the head of North America DSO relationships. Another was VP of sales for North America.

I daydreamed about what a partnership could mean for Implant Ninja. I was really optimistic about where this might go.

They asked me to help them develop an online mentorship pathway. A way to combine online training with hands on training and mentorship.

I gave all of them access to the entire Implant Ninja platform. And I outlined exactly how we could develop this online coaching system. I spent early mornings and late nights thinking up the curriculum and the pathway for mentorship. I was so excited. *Finally*, I thought, a big implant company notices that we are doing something worthy. Along with the mentorship platform, I wanted to help them re-create their customer experience. Maybe I would finally get to enact some of those much needed changes within the implant industry, I thought.

As I explained the online mentorship program to the group, everyone around the table seemed really happy with my suggestions and eagerly took notes. The each shook my hand and said that they were looking forward to seeing this move forward. And that I should expect to hear back soon.

This whole process dragged on for months after months. I wondered when it would come to fruition.

Then, I got an email.

It was a mass marketing email announcing this big implant company's new online mentorship program.

They were launching it without me.

My initial thought was that this was just a simple mistake. I didn't want to think of the possibility that maybe, I had just been taken advantage of.

I emailed them right away and asked kindly what the hell was going on. They reassured me it was nothing to worry about.

But then, they said they valued our partnership at $25,000 and I could take it or leave it.

I badly wanted a partnership. Maybe because it was a validation, that we were onto something. That we were building something valuable.

But not like this. $25,000 felt like a slap in the face. A kick in the groin.

I didn't allow myself to wonder if they had ripped me off. I didn't want to let myself get angry or resentful.

Then, the person that I was working on that deal with decided to quit the implant company to join Smile Direct Club (an emerging ortho company) instead.

And my deal died with her departure.

I've shared our platform with a handful of hundred-million-dollar and billion-dollar businesses. They have never resulted in any deal. But they were always eager to see what was under the hood.

Deal dead, I turned my attention back to my online business. And it wasn't looking so good.

The immediate impact of COVID was that our sales dropped by 70% in the first quarter.

Alarms went off in my head.

Was this it? Did our little project come to an end?

I'm not a patient person. In the face of emergencies, this becomes cartoonishly evident.

One time, at my parent's office, the toaster caught fire. It enveloped Teresa's bagel as the flames climbed up towards the cabinets. As Teresa stood there, I imagined the flames burning down all of my parents' hard work. So, I grabbed the watercooler, ripped it off its stand and hoisted it above the flames. The water wouldn't come out of the barrel.

I had badly damaged the watercooler. And the flames continued.

Teresa walked over quietly and sprayed the fire extinguisher over the flames.

In building Implant Ninja, there are moments where everything is working, and we are growing, and everyone is happy.

But then there are fires.

And I have to control myself from over-reacting to them. Pivoting is sometimes necessary, but in my overactive and extreme mind, I immediately come up with 5 crazy ways to put out the fire, when sometimes what is needed is to sit and think for a moment and grab the extinguisher.

The five of us worked in that little 450 square foot space. We turned into a real team during that phase. We were scrappy, but were able to jointly brainstorm and evolve the brand.

We became fixated on our new mission:

Making dental implants simple.

That was also the time when my home life changed forever.

It had always been just the 3 of us: Me, Teresa, and Olivia. But on May 4th (*May the fourth be with you*) our little Charlotte Abigail Chicchon was born.

Her birth was the opposite of Olivia's. She was delivered via cesarian section in under one hour.

She came out smiling. And that smile has never left her face.

While Teresa and I were terrified that we were bringing another child into this hurricane of a world, she was the perfect counterbalance for all our family's strife.

In her, Olivia found a best friend.

And Teresa found her peace.

During this little peaceful intermission, I bought a boat.

It was a little beat-up, rusty aluminum thing I picked up from a garage sale for $100. While Teresa nursed Charlotte, Olivia and I spent a couple of days fixing up the boat.

When it was freshly sanded and painted, we took it out for a ride with my dad on the Delta River by our house.

As we rowed along, the breeze was a welcome respite from the oppressive Central Valley heat. The temperature was already in the hundreds by then.

My dad watched me through his sunglasses, and then he said something I had been waiting to hear for a very long time.

"Now I understand what you were building all this time. It was so smart to do your online courses before Olivia's surgery. You guys would have been in serious financial trouble."

Then he said,

"I am proud of you, my son. You did really good for your family."

We took turns rowing the boat down the river.

A sea otter popped it's head out of the water, to Olivia's delight.

Beyond the fields of dry grass, a yellow airplane flew over an orchard in the distance.

As the breeze hit my face, I breathed it in.

This is what success must feel like, I thought to myself.

For the moment, all was right in our world.

CHAPTER 13

Then it all started to change.

First, it was all over social media. Riots and looting breaking out across the country. It was reported that people in a Facebook group in Stockton were planning to go door to door and cause damage and loot in my neighborhood soon.

I thought of baby Charlotte. Then, I thought of buying a gun.

But, as I had no experience or training, I was sure it would actually be *more* dangerous to for me to have one in my home. So, I bought bear mace and hard plastic batons.

The four of us did practice drills in which Teresa and the girls would run to the bathroom. We told Olivia she would have to lock herself in a small compartment of the bathroom, but she shot back, "If someone comes in here, I'll take this stick and poke them in the eyes!!"

I stayed up at night waiting and listening. Evening gunshots are not an uncommon sound in Stockton, California. But their echo was just a bit more ominous in those nights.

One restless night, I had a dream that it was the end of times. Asteroids were crashing down all around us. Woken up from my sleep, I thought maybe the trash trucks outside were making the menacing crashing noise from my dream. But when I looked outside the sky was red. Then I heard the crashing sound again. It was thunder. The red sky and roar of thunder at 6AM, felt unreal. I thought I might still be dreaming.

The news said that everyone should stay indoors. Lightning had struck around Napa and some areas in Southern California, and now fires were spreading all across the state. A thick cloud of orange-red smoke lingered and we were told that the fires were coming our way. On our phones, the air quality said *"HAZARDOUS TO HEALTH, everyone should avoid being outside."*

It felt like the world was going to hell in a handbasket. The sweltering heat wave, the riots, businesses closing all around us, our revenue going up and down, Donald Trump constantly on the TV saying things that seemed to fan the flames of social unrest, the outward aggression in the streets, and now the orange sky.

There was so much uncertainty.

And in uncertain times, I scramble.

I decided this is it.

If the world *is*, in fact, going to hell, then there's no better time than now to start my implant company. The one that I had been wanting to start but had been too broke. Too unstable.

Who knew what the future will bring? I knew that I needed to go all in, now.

So, I talked it over with Teresa. She knew this had been my dream for so long. She was all in too.

And with her full support, our team jumped into creating what we would call Implant Club. We were finally starting our own implant company.

We needed to address all of those shortcomings and frustrations that I had encountered in my implant journey. I announced what I was up to on Instagram, and then I got to work.

Then, one early morning, while I was writing on my laptop, I heard a shriek coming from Olivia's room. This wasn't uncommon. She was always afraid of being alone.

But when I leapt up the stairs and ran into her room to comfort her, she was pointing at a small pool of blood soaked into her pillow.

"It's okay hunny. Were you scared?" I tried to reassure her.

"I'm scared if you are, daddy." She looked at my eyes to see if there was fear.

From then on, every so often, she would have blood in her mouth in the mornings.

Sometimes she didn't notice until she brushed her teeth and the bubbles were bright red. And she would quickly spit it all out in terror.

We called her doctors in Seattle, and they advised us to try an experimental medication—a chemotherapy that was used for breast cancer. Her doctor was hopeful that it would help control Olivia's condition. The issue was that, because it was experimental, she would need several tests and appointments before she could start because we were out-of-state. It could take months to get our hands on it.

Then, one morning the pool of blood was too much for me to bear. I couldn't stand seeing the look of despair in Olivia's eyes as she wondered what was happening to her.

I jumped into 'emergency Ivan' mode. And tried to find our footing for this next scramble.

Taking her to the ER in Stockton was not an option. They wouldn't know about her condition. They wouldn't have the best care for her.

I told Teresa, "Let's just get the hell out of here. Let's go to Washington."

"I'll load up the car, let's get out of here by 1PM." She shot back without hesitation.

If we were physically present, living there in Washington, it would expedite Olivia's start of the medication.

We packed the car and the four of us made the 13-hour journey to Bellevue, Washington.

CHAPTER 14

After making that trip to Washington in 2021, we didn't return to Cali.

Instead, overtaken by my sense of responsibility for helping Olivia 'get better,' I insisted that we stay in Washington indefinitely.

We were in a state of confusion as a family. We were sleep deprived. And with all the new changes and stressors, I was feeling quite unstable. I couldn't think. I couldn't reason. So, I tried desperately to fix the situation.

The nightmare that I wanted to avoid at all costs was for my little Olivia to have a complication while we were in Stockton because we would not have a reliable hospital to take her to. The hospitals within 1 hour of Stockton are average. They are fine for routine care, delivering a baby, and regular emergency treatment.

But they didn't have world class doctors that specialize in Lymphatic Malformations. Most doctors have never dealt with Olivia's condition before. And some have mistaken her mass for an infection. There was just too much that could go wrong in an emergency situation with doctors unfamiliar with her condition.

With so much out of my control, I grasped at the things that I could control.

I kept thinking,

If Olivia has an emergency, we will be only 5 minutes from the best hospital in the country for her. If we are here, we are safe.

I became fixated on that—and I didn't want to let it go.

Teresa felt we should stay in Washington until things settled down. A month, maybe two months. But I savagely held on to my "If we are here, we are safe" mentality. I pushed for staying in Washington permanently.

I was scared. And scared people behave rashly.

Seeing that I was afraid and not wanting to fight, Teresa relented. We took a shotgun approach to finding an apartment. We looked at 7 places in one day, and picked the 7th one. In a matter of 2 weeks we were all settled in.

After all the pre-requisite blood tests, we arrived at the familiar halls of the Seattle Children's Hospital for Olivia to start her experimental medication.

The doctor handed me a white bottle with a big, highlighter-yellow sticker on it that read "HAZARDOUS DRUG."

We had missed the deadline for the clinical trial, so that meant we would have to pay out of pocket.

I took a little pink pill in my hand.

"How could this tiny pink tablet be so HAZARDOUS?," I found myself thinking.

It was a chemotherapy medication used for breast cancer. In that moment, I became afraid.

As I stared at the pill, I considered running out of the clinic. I thought of cancelling the whole thing. Of picking up Olivia and escaping.

Then I lowered my hand to Olivia.

"Here hunny, this is your medicine. Go ahead and swallow it." I tried to look confident as I said this.

Looked at the pill. Then back at me. And she said, "Okay daddy, I trust you." And she swallowed it.

We were hopeful that the medication would help Oli. But we were also worried about the side effects. First, Olivia started complaining about her heart. She said it hurt. She said it was beating too fast. And then she started to become pale and weak again.

Then, began the fits of rage. Out of nowhere Olivia would charge at us, full of anger, swinging her arms.

As she screamed, blood would spray out of her mouth.

I was convinced, by this time, that only one thing would calm Olivia's rage—nature. So, I took Charlie and Olivia out every single day to play at the beach or to do a short hike in the woods. It soothed Olivia, unlike any medicine ever could. Watching the children play without a care in the world, was the happiest I had ever felt.

So, I tried to alternate between being a superhero for my kids and running Implant Ninja.

Again, in an effort to find a way to finance Olivia's healthcare and for our stay in Washington, that week I finalized an implant book I had been putting together for a few months called the Little Book of Implant Wisdom.

It immediately sold out.

Our Implant Ninja fans bailed us out, we would be able to pay for our apartment.

But again, the person who was forgotten was Teresa.

While I was focused on taking the kids out to have fun, Teresa was the one who ultimately cared for them 24/7. She cooked, cleaned, got them ready for the day, put them to bed, and watched them while I snuck out to put in work for Implant Ninja.

She was quietly there, making sure we had everything we needed to care for our children.

In an instant, her life had been completely changed. No family. No friends. No familiar routine. She was unhappy. But she never complained.

That entire year was delirium.

But Washington had been some respite. It was a safe space for Olivia and Charlie.

But Olivia's PTSD continued to plague us. Also, benign-sounding side-effect of the medication was turning out to be harder to manage than we thought. The medication made her uncontrollably itchy. Which meant that we woke up every 2 hours at night, every night.

Which meant that Olivia was always tired and angry. And it seemed like it would never get better.

We desperately needed help.

Teresa wanted to be around our family. Grandparents, brothers, sisters. She insisted that the kids needed to know their family.

"We've just been through a really traumatic time. We need some time together too." She said.

So, after 6 months, we packed up moved back to our hometown of Stockton, California—where we had help and community.

But where there was no nature to ease Olivia's rage. Or was it within me that the rage lived on? I couldn't tell anymore.

I just knew that my encounters with Olivia always left me disheartened and empty.

Feeling totally impotent, I fell into a deep depression. I blamed my surroundings. My city. I suddenly hated everything about Stockton. The schools, the restaurants, the crime, the homeless villages, the lack of trees. I hated it all.

As was my pattern, I rashly suggested we move back to Washington. After enough of my bitching, Teresa agreed to make the trip back to Washington to give it one last shot.

But we belonged neither here nor there. We were nomads.

We couldn't agree on how to move forward. On where to settle down. I wanted to be near nature and Olivia's hospital. Teresa wanted us to be near family. We were lost in our confusion.

Earlier that year, we had flown to Stockton to celebrate my nephew's baptism. Like me, my sister had married her high school sweetheart, Jonathan Canton. And they now had a beautiful little boy whom they were having baptized.

My whole family attended, but at the close of the ceremony, my grandfather got a stomachache and left. The next week, he was diagnosed with cancer.

Over the next 4 months, we watched him wither to nothing. And then, it was over.

The man who had taught me about logic, about history, who had recounted the stories of the Incas... was no more.

I gave a speech at his funeral. About family. About how we all carry on the characteristics, the mannerisms, of our relatives long since past. About how they live on within us.

Months passed, but his absence didn't yet sink in.

Not until this point. This point in which I was totally lost and needed his counsel. But I could never have it. He was gone.

I felt like I would run into him at any moment. That I might find him sweeping leaves in my backyard. Or reading a book in the kitchen in the early hours of the morning.

But I didn't. And the desperate inability to communicate with him, overwhelmed me.

I wanted to ask him what I should do. What the right family decisions were. How to be a *strong* man.

But I couldn't, and so I fell further into despair. A dark cloud hung over me. And it was painfully evident to all around me.

One night, Teresa was a bit quiet at the dinner table. I pressed her to tell me what was wrong.

"You know…" tears began to well in her eyes, "one day I will die too!

"But I'm still here now! Waiting for you!

"I'm ready to enjoy life with you! I know we've been dealt a shitty hand these last 4 years, but I can't live the rest of my life like this.

"I need to have peace. I need stability.

"You focus so much on being a great dad and providing for us, but don't you see that I need you too!!?"

For the first time in a very long time, I looked back on my actions from Teresa's point of view. And I realized what I had been doing to her.

CHAPTER 15

My whole life I've been seeking something. Something that I had felt was missing.

Something that I needed, as a pre-requisite to be happy. And without it, I couldn't be peaceful.

I couldn't be stable.

And I wouldn't allow myself to be happy until I attained this elusive accomplishment.

You could hear it when I spoke of the beach house I would someday own in Hawaii.

Or when I spoke of the day when our implant business finally took off.

Or when I yearned longingly for the moment when Olivia would finally be healthy and peaceful.

Many people go their whole lives chasing an elusive goal. Chronically discontent with what they currently have.

To them, the proverbial grass is always greener on the other side. And throughout their entire life, they are always *almost there*.

They might think,

Just a few more years of hustle, and I'll be happy.

Just have to finish my degree, and I'll be set.

I just have to pass this test, and I'll be stress free.

Just another thing, and I'll finally allow myself to breathe.

…or at least that's what they tell themselves.

These feelings, stem from insecurity.

Insecurity is a powerful motivator. It can push you to accomplish great things. But it will never allow you to be happy. No accomplishment will ever be enough to satiate that beast.

For the past decade, I had been driven by insecurity and *fear*. Fear from owing almost $1 Million dollars in student debt. Fear for my daughter's health. And the ever-present fear that I was going about everything the wrong way and that I was not enough.

I feared that I would never achieve that *stability* that Teresa had requested before we had gotten married.

Both fear and insecurity are powerful drivers. But they will never lead to fulfillment or stability.

I sat on the curb in front of my driveway at our home in Stockton.

Charlie was pushing a pink stroller with a small baby doll who was going along for the ride. When the stroller got stuck on a twig, or a crack the baby would tip over and Charlie would say, "Ooops!" and put the baby back in the seat.

Olivia, with a blue helmet and knee and elbow pads, was riding her bike around the court, ringing a bell on the handlebar as she went.

Then both kids ran over to a neighbor's front lawn, apparently having spotted some lizard or slug in the bush. I watched as Olivia ran around pointing at things and explaining to Charlotte the intricacies of all the critters that live in the yards.

With Charlotte now almost 2 years old, they had become best friends. They were inseparable.

Teresa walked peacefully after them in a red spring dress. She looked back at me and gave me a tired-but-happy smile. The sunlight peeked from behind a tree, making the leaves glow and casting a golden backdrop on Teresa's long, brown hair.

I took all of this in.

I had spent so many years running away from instability and chasing a *future* happiness and *future* success, that I hadn't realized that I already had a beautiful and wonderful life.

That—*as it was*—I was completely fulfilled.

I had been postponing my happiness and dragging Teresa along for the ride. But no more.

I learned to live my life, being fulfilled in the present. And being happy with myself *as I was*.

And I completely changed my outlook on goal setting.

My old way of thinking was:

"My business will be successful, and I will bust my ass until it is."

Or

"I need to find a way to pay this off or else!"

But my new mentality became,

"I will hustle because I enjoy it. I love the creative process of my work. And it makes me feel good to have a solid work ethic."

Having this mindset, is much more effective. Rather than fear or insecurity as motivators, what drives you is the fun and creativity. You are propelled by the excitement.

This inherently leads you towards "success" or more revenue. But the important point is that "success" or revenue is NOT the goal per se.

The goal is just to enjoy the process. And if you truly enjoy the process, then good things will come.

I carried this over to my personal life. Instead of coveting a life I would someday have, I began focusing on living a daily life I could be proud of. On being a person I could be proud of on a daily basis. And enjoying the journey.

I didn't get there all by myself. My wife and parents helped me with this mindset reboot.

Also, a few books helped me along the way: Shoe Dog by the founder of Nike, Twelve and a Half by Gary Vaynerchuck, and Zen Mind Beginners Mind by Shunryu Suzuki.

But by the end of it, I had a profound sense of calm—of non-urgency. I no longer carried that uncontrolled anger around with me.

For the first time since I could remember, I felt...peaceful. It was so foreign to me that I didn't recognize it. I no longer felt like I had to prove myself to anyone. I no longer had to prove my manhood to myself.

I was already a man that I could be proud of.

It was then that I realized something profound.

I realized that I AM a badass. I have been a badass. Ever since I set out to be. Ever since I was that little kid on the blacktop.

I have never needed anyone else's validation.

I was enough, just as I was. Just as I am.

And from that moment on, I became invincible.

I was able to enjoy my life. And, not feeling the overwhelming pressure to succeed, I finally allowed myself to develop a fulfilling relationship with Teresa. In addition to husband and wife, we were now partners and friends.

It finally felt like I found *stability*.

With my mindset completely changed, I was ready to get back to work.

I got focused on continuing to grow our online educational platform and to get ready to launch the "early user" testing phase of our implant system, Implant Club. I did the work not because I felt that I *had* to. I did it because I loved the process. This is who I was.

Then, one morning, I got a call...

"Hello, is this the Implant Ninja? This is THE CEO."

The CEO?

Could it be?

The very person who's story had inspired me to dream big and become an implant industry badass?

"I saw one of the videos you made using my implants. I forwarded it to the Straumann CEO. I wanted to show him that you think mine is better." His voice broke into a chuckle.

I was thrilled and nervous to be talking to the man who was responsible for so much of the progress of the implant industry. I told him about Implant Ninja, my teaching adventures, and about how I planned to start my own implant company.

Then, the conversation took an immediate turn.

"Why do you want to sell implants?" He sounded amused.

I told him about my dream.

"How old are you? You're too young to start an implant company. You're like a baby who want a pony."

He continued,

"Listen, if you get into starting your own implant company…YOU'RE GOING TO LOSE YOUR ASS. I'm making a comeback, and I'm going to beat everybody. I will be THE LAST MAN STANDING."

I thanked him for calling me. And ended the call.

He followed up with an email. Telling me that I don't have enough money to start an implant company.

He sent me a picture of his Rolls Royce.

Then he sent a picture of his private jet. He literally had an airplane fly next to his jet so that he could have a photo of it in the sky.

I was stunned. This person, who I had idolized since dental school, who I aspired to be like, was ridiculing me.

He told me I would lose my ass.

Then, I smiled.

This would be fun.

Nothing like a good fight to get your blood pumping.

The adrenaline kicked in. Only this time, I felt like I could control it.

I grabbed my blue expo marker.

Sat in front of my whiteboard.

And planned our next moves.

A HUGE shoutout to all my friends and supporters. The following folks participated in our initial launch of Screw Dog! Thanks for having my back!

Gloria Martin	Henry Kendrick
Jairo Barrera	Navtej Atwal
Baljit Dhillon	Priya Patel
Forrest Newman	Kevin Kem
Jackson Call	Mirette Boushra
Mary Rondeau	Michael Starbody
Dan Ellingson	Jesse Elledge
Roberto Gallardo	Roderick Kim
Samuel Conti III	Mohamed Abdel Hakim
Madai Perez	Gregg Vesta
Justin Joseph	Laura Pogosian
Samer Elbatanouny	Amanda Farley
Geraldine O'Mara	Sara Mandell
Nick Dargel	Andy Cheung
Kevin Poupore	Diego Sanchez
Rayan Ghandour	Nikola Skakavac
William Manolarakis	Nathan Wu
Stephanie Settimi	Kaleb Davis
Mary Bennardi	David Wong
Joelle Hirschfeld	Steven Yu Wen Lin
Geetha Vani Ommi	Steven Truman
Ivan Ruvalcaba	Sadaf Assadi
Joshua Heyrend	Diana Huynh
Rooshika Dalaya	Bhumika Patel
Darin Throndson	Taylor Eiford
Mohammed Jabbar	Kimberly Kershaw
Ed Torres	Eric Kessler
Luke Czer	Thomas Cooner
Sam King	Laszlo Rivero Prince
Kevin Choi	Sheldon Lu
Kenneth Nguyen	Partha Mukherji
Darryl Torculas	Chase Culbertson

Henry Troung
Neha Arora
Hannah Tsai
Randall Jones
Wissam Ayoub
Christian Lopez
Chet Singh
David Fisher
Hammad Shere
Tuan Anh Ta
Avi Patel
Gary Holtzclaw
Nikhil Patel
Tyler Kemerer
Isaac Shuster
Jordynn Pozzuto
Jonathan Locke
Danny Pazos
Jenny Perkins
Charlene Ramos
Villanueva
Joel Sinervo
Brandon Morales
Dustin Nadeau
Samuel Cho
Apexa Mehta
Micael Hilario
Scott Carr
Chanon Ruangjumrusvet
Nicolas Didier
Ramsey Warner
Rayan Al Edreesi
Sae-Ho Chun
Melissa Loftin
Anna Coyne
Jason Gopaul

Kamran Pakdamanian
Assad Qasim
Ian Lin
Mary Bennardi
Sam Schmidt
Alison Scott
Bo Ram Um
Austin Hartford
Derek Weigand
Shaman Hamed
Albert Ilyayev
Christopher Kurimoto
Chandler Conner
Todd Larrabee
Blake Ferando
Gurki Malhi
Clifford Young
Paul Falvey
Jerrin Johnson
Ian Lin
Sarah Clayton
Nathan Pinsky
Ryan Rupert
John Yacoub
Aman Kumar
Andy Burton
Cherry Harika
Katherine Leung
Nathan Mitchell
Andre Paredes
David Abeyounis
Greg Pisotti
Brad Jurgenmeier
Kyle Hargis
Anthony Adams
Daniel Salazar

Jeffrey Standage
Acey Nixon
Richard Wong
David Alpert
Ryan Rhodes
Ramon Chicchon
Herschel Ungar
Jonnathan Matute
Christian Watkins
Emma Yang
Michael Indig
Christofer Hatzis
Randall Jones
Saurabh Sharma
Dustin Kruse
Henry Jackson Jr
Kevin Jones
Juan Santos
Brandon Thai

Khiem Tran
Ryan Borders
Andrew Pak
Alan Cho
Nels Hvass L.D.
Fred Blum
Victor Miranda
Evelyn Herrera
Claire Sesson
Cynthia Co Ting Keh
Yong Woong Lee
Steven Alvarado
Calvin Huen
Jared Castro
Ammera Kaing Martin
Jennifer Vitez
Jeff Buizastrow
Margaret Porter
Mohammed Ismail

ABOUT THE AUTHOR

Ivan Chicchon is the founder of Implant Ninja, an online education platform and Implant Club, a dental implant company.

Both companies aim to keep implants simple and make people happy.

Follow his story on Instagram at @implant_ninja.

You can learn more about Implant Ninja's online courses at:

www.implantninja.com

You can learn more about his implant company at

www.theimplantclub.com

Made in the USA
Monee, IL
09 February 2023

27397541R00085